Progress in Reading Assessment

for years 3 t

Colin McCarty
Kate Ruttle

STAGE TWO MANUAL

HODDER EDUCATION
AN HACHETTE UK COMPANY

Copyright acknowlegements

The authors and publishers wish to thank the following for permission to include copyright material in the *PiRA* tests:

Andrew Fusek Peters for the poem 'Mum' from *Sadderday and Funday*, first published in the UK by Hodder Children's, an imprint of Hachette Children's Books, 338 Euston Road, London NW1 3BH *(in PiRA 3 Autumn)*; Valerie Bloom and Eddison Pearson Ltd for the poem 'Time', from *The World is Sweet*, published by Bloomsbury Children's Books *(in PiRA 4 Autumn)*; Lois Simmie for the poem 'Attic Fanatic', from *Auntie's Knitting a Baby*, published by Douglas and Mcintyre *(in PiRA 4 Spring)*; Geraldine McCaughrean and David Higham Associates for the adapted extract from *Crossing the Canyon*, published by Bloomsbury Children's Books *(in PiRA 5 Autumn)*; Great Ormond Street Hospital Children's Charity for 'The Pirate Crew', adapted from *Peter Pan*, by J. M. Barrie *(in PiRA 5 Summer)*; Professor Meic Stephens for the poem 'Merlin and the Snake's Egg', by Leslie Norris, from *The Oxford Book of Story Poems* (OUP) *(in PiRA 6 Spring)*.

Orders: please contact Bookpoint Ltd, 130 Milton Park, Abingdon, Oxon OX14 4SB. Telephone: (44) 01235 827827. Fax: (44) 01235 400401. Lines are open 9.00–5.00, Monday to Saturday, with a 24-hour message answering service. Visit our website at www.hoddereducation.co.uk

Copyright © 2010 Hodder and Stoughton Limited
First published in 2010 by Hodder Education, an Hachette UK company, 338 Euston Road, London NW1 3BH

Impression number   8
Year   2014 2013

All rights reserved. Apart from any use permitted under UK copyright law, no part of this publication may be reproduced or transmitted in any form or by any means, electronic or mechanical, including photocopying and recording, or held within any information storage and retrieval system, without permission in writing from the publisher. This publication is excluded from the reprographic licensing scheme administered by the Copyright Licensing Agency Ltd.

Printed in England by Hobbs the Printers Ltd, Totton, Hampshire SO40 3WX.

A catalogue record for this title is available from the British Library

ISBN 978 1 444 11119 4

PiRA

Contents

1 Introduction — 5
  Why use *PiRA*? — 5
  Purposes and uses of the *PiRA* tests — 6
  Using *PiRA* at Key Stage 2 — 7

2 Administering the *PiRA* Tests — 9
  Giving the tests — 9
  Marking and recording results — 10
  The *PiRA* Record Sheet (*photocopiable*) — 11

3 Obtaining and Interpreting Test Scores — 13
  Standardised scores and percentiles — 13
  Reading ages and NC levels — 16
  Reporting progress: the *PiRA* Scale — 16
  Predicting future performance — 20
  Diagnostic and formative interpretation — 25
  Three case studies — 26

4 Technical Information — 30

5 Answers and Mark Schemes — 35
  PiRA 3 — 35
  PiRA 4 — 41
  PiRA 5 — 49
  PiRA 6 — 57

Standardised Score conversion tables — 66
  PiRA 3 — 66
  PiRA 4 — 72
  PiRA 5 — 78
  PiRA 6 — 84

Appendix A: Levels of demand and AF coverage for each test — 90

Appendix B: Facilities for each question — 92

Appendix C: Mean marks by sub-level — 95

Acknowledgements

It was a team effort that created and developed the suite of twenty *PiRA* reading tests:

- The major author was Kate Ruttle. She wrote the fourteen tests from Reception year to the end of Year 4 and worked with Colin McCarty in the design, editing and evolution of all the assessments and mark schemes.
- Marie Lallaway wrote the six tests for Years 5 and 6.
- Mig Bennett wrote the playscripts for Years 3, 4, 5 and 6.
- Lorna Pepper advised on the quality and demand of all the texts and questions.
- Viv Kilburn was the language consultant.
- Jane Swift was the artist.
- Tony Kiek worked with Colin McCarty to undertake the statistical analyses and produce the standardised scores and target-setting predictions from the marks obtained in the trials.
- Colin McCarty designed the suite of tests, together with the predictive and diagnostic information for teachers, working closely with Chas Knight, the publisher at Hodder, to present tests, mark schemes and information in easy-to-use forms.

Our sincere thanks go to the staff of the following schools, who administered the testing and marked the scripts, and the many thousands of pupils who took the assessments each term.

Beck Row Primary School, Beck Row, IP28 8AE
Bishopsteignton Primary School, Teignmouth, TQ14 9RJ
Bowbridge Primary School, Newark, NG24 4EP
Chesterton Primary School, Newcastle, ST5 5NT
Cheveley C of E Primary School, Cheveley, CB8 9DF
College Heath Middle School, Mildenhall, IP28 7PT
Cranberry Primary School, Alsager, ST7 2LE
Ellington Primary School, Maidenhead, SL6 7JA
Featherby Junior School, Gillingham, ME8 9RN
Four Oaks Primary School, Sutton Coldfield, B74 4PA
Grange Park Primary School, Enfield, N21 1PP
Great Heath Primary School, Mildenhall, IP28 7NX
Great Linford Primary School, Great Linford, MK14 5BL
Great Wood Primary School, Upper Tean, ST10 4JY
Hambridge Community Primary School, Langport, TA10 0AZ
Holy Cross R C Primary School, Catford, SE6 2LD
Horsendale Primary School, Nottingham, NG16 1AP
Lakenheath Primary School, Lakenheath, IP27 9DU
Larkholme Primary School, Fleetwood, FY7 8QB
Larks Hill J and I School, Pontefract, WF8 4RJ
Lower Darwen Primary School, Lower Darwen, BB3 0RB
Malmesbury Primary School, Malmsbury, SN16 9JR
Monkfield Park Primary School, Cambourne, CB23 5AX

Much Marcle C of E Primary School, Ledbury, HR8 2LY
New Christchurch C of E Primary School, Reading, RG2 0AY
Nonsuch Primary School, Birmingham, B32 3SE
Palace Wood Primary School, Allington, ME16 0HB
Parkstone Primary School, Hull, HU6 7DE
Pokesdown Primary School, Bournemouth, BH5 2AS
Pottery Primary School, Belper, DE56 1HA
Queensbridge Primary School, Farnworth, BL4 7BL
Sacred Heart R C Primary School, Sowerby Bridge, HX6 1BL
Scaltback Middle School, Newmarket, CB8 0DJ
Seascale Primary School, Seascale, CA20 1LZ
St Jame's C of E Primary School, Handsworth, B21 8NH
St Mary's C of E Primary School, Mildenhall, IP28 7AB
St Peter's C of E Combined School, Burnham, SL1 7DE
Swaythling Primary School, Southampton, SO17 3SZ
Tuddenham C of E Primary School, Tuddenham St Mary, IP28 6SA
Victoria Road Primary School, St Budeaux, PL5 2RH
West Row Primary School, West Row, IP28 8NY
Wharton Primary School, Little Hulton, M38 9XA
Whiston Willis Primary School, Prescot, L35 2XY
Woodside Primary School, Little Thurrock, RM16 2GJ
Worlaby Primary School, Brigg, DN20 0NA
Yewdale Primary School, Carlisle, CA2 7SD

PiRA — Introduction

Progress in Reading Assessment (PiRA) is a suite of tests designed to be used at three points in each primary school year, to measure and monitor pupils' progress term by term, and to provide reliable, predictive and diagnostic information.

A separate test is available for autumn, spring and summer terms for Years 1–6, and for the spring and summer terms in Reception.

PiRA is designed for whole-class use, with pupils of all abilities. The test booklets are simple and quick to administer – each test takes a maximum 50 minutes – and straightforward to mark.

The tests provide a wide, thorough coverage at each level within the National Curriculum, from Reception to Year 6. This has been assured by systematically sampling appropriate aspects of the literacy curriculum and *Assessing Pupil Progress* (APP) in accordance with national guidelines for each Year.

Why use *PiRA*?

PiRA gives reliable **summative** information. For example:

- if you want to follow the progress of your pupils from term to term, as well as year to year through the primary school, *PiRA* – uniquely – provides *three* carefully designed tests for each year;
- if you need to establish a National Curriculum level for each pupil, *PiRA* tests are calibrated to indicate National Curriculum levels which are further subdivided into upper, middle and lower – a, b and c – to provide a finer level of information;
- if you wish to use a test to support APP, *PiRA* tests are also calibrated to indicate levels subdivided into high, secure and low – H, S and L;
- if you wish to set appropriate and meaningful targets for your pupils, and to evaluate their progress, *PiRA* tests provide an empirical basis on which to do so;
- if you need to have an external reference for your value-added requirements, *PiRA* tests supply it.

Also, because it has a **diagnostic** capability, *PiRA* enables you to investigate some of the strengths and weaknesses of your pupils' reading skills.

To enable you to use the information in a diagnostic/formative way, total scores can be broken down into distinct aspects of reading, giving a useful **profile** which reflects the Assessment Focuses (AFs) which are defined within APP. Across the *PiRA* series as a whole, these are

- Phonics (AF1)
- Literal comprehension (AF2)
- Reading for meaning (AF3)
- Appreciation of reading (AFs 4–7)

The balance of the questions assessing these at each level obviously changes as the tests become more demanding, helping to pinpoint where pupils may be under-performing.

PiRA systematically assesses pupils' reading of different **text types** or **genres** – fiction, various forms of non-fiction, poetry and playscripts – in line with national guidelines across the primary phase.

You can also examine the performance of pupils on *each question* – using the percentage of pupils that answered each question correctly in the national standardisation (technically, the *facility value*), you can easily compare the performance of your own pupils with those in the national sample.

In short, *PiRA* will help you to answer parents, governors, inspectors or headteachers who ask:

- How has *my* child done compared to others of his or her age or year group?
- What sort of pattern of performance do pupils in a particular year typically achieve?
- Has this pupil made good progress from year to year?
- What would be a reasonable level of achievement for this pupil next term?
- What are the strengths or successes of this pupil, or the class?
- What individual and class *targets* are appropriate and realistic?
- On what aspects of reading should this pupil focus to maximise progress?
- What would constitute good, average or poor progress for this pupil or class?

This manual contains all the information you need to obtain NC and APP levels, reading ages and profile measures, as well as standardised scores, giving a wealth of information that will enable you to be more effective in managing learning in your classroom.

By using the *optional* **PiRA Digital** CD-ROM, you can unlock even more diagnostic information. If you are using the pencil-and-paper tests, this digital resource lets you analyse *group* performance (eg by class and/or gender), track pupil performance through the school and generate individual progress predictions. And if you want some or all of your pupil year groups to take the tests on-screen, in full colour, **PiRA Digital** provides that fully interactive option.

Purposes and uses of the *PiRA* tests

PiRA provides a *standardised* assessment of a pupil's reading attainment. It also provides a *profile* (see below) which helps you to identify those pupils who may need further teaching and practice.

For each pupil, *PiRA* gives three 'global' measures of reading attainment:

- **standardised score** (from which a **percentile** can be derived);
- **reading age**;
- **national curriculum and APP level** and sub-level.

Each test also gives a **points score** (widely used by local authorities).

The *PiRA* test results have been statistically linked from term to term and year to year to show a clear set of information, enabling you to monitor strengths and weaknesses and track progress through the whole primary phase, while also enabling quite detailed comparisons of individual patterns of performance against the norms and patterns for the term or year.

Underpinning all this – and arguably the most useful single measure of all – is the **PiRA Scale**: this gives a decimalised level which enables you to monitor small increments of progress from term to term.

The *PiRA* Scale acts as a common 'spine' on which are plotted all of the *PiRA* tests across the whole primary phase (Table 3.5 on pages 18–19 shows this scale across Key Stage 2). It provides the statistical basis for *predicting* pupil progress and future attainment, based on the termly performance data of over 10,000 pupils nationally.

The **profile** may be completed on the front cover of the pupil's test paper. Do this by using the code letters (see page 10) alongside each mark in the test paper to allow you to collate the pupil's performance against assessment guidelines.

The photocopiable **PiRA record sheet** on pages 11–12 lets you plot the profile scores and view progress relative to national average performance (shown by the tints) for each aspect of reading.

By completing a profile for each pupil you can build a picture of each pupil's performances that will let you follow progress and provide a set of validated data for future years.

If you wish, you can also average your pupils' scores to create an overall *class* profile. The pattern revealed may inform both teaching and target-setting, as it will highlight the reading skills in which pupils are secure or confident and those that need addressing. Alternatively input the profile scores into **PiRA Digital** and the software will do all of this for you.

Assessing weaker readers

The spread of the tests – as shown in Table 1.1 – allows you to use each test with wide-ability groups, including weaker readers, and allows all pupils to experience some success.

Very poor readers may benefit from taking tests for 'younger' terms or years, where they are more likely to experience success and be able to demonstrate what they know and understand, rather than struggle with texts that are too demanding for them. A number of schools in the trials adopted this policy. Table 1.1 shows the pattern of demand of each test, which you can use to select a test that should allow the poorer reader some success and yet still meet some questions that will challenge him or her. In a similar way, able pupils following an accelerated pathway may take 'older age group' tests.

Note that it may not be possible to obtain a standardised score or percentile when the tests are used in this way, if the pupil is outside the chronological age range of the conversion table for the test used. You will be able to get a National Curriculum and APP sub-level and reading age, however, as well as a *PiRA* Scale score.

Using *PiRA* at Key Stage 2

PiRA can, if necessary, be used just once every year, but is much more informative if used termly. At Key Stage 2, each test contains 40 marks and is based on varied pieces of reading material, following, as a guide, the work for each term recommended in national guidelines as well as developing on from Key Stage 1.

The most important reading 'assessment focuses' for children in the early stages of reading are decoding text (AF1) and making meaning – that is, literal comprehension (AF2). As children continue to develop as readers, inferencing (AF3) becomes more prominent. More subtle reading skills (AFs 4–7: see Appendix A) are less critical at the initial and early stages, and less central to developing reading *per se*. For this reason, *PiRA* analyses conflate AFs 4–7 and report these under the heading *Appreciation of Reading*.

The Key Stage 2 *PiRA* tests therefore profile the core skills that underpin progress in reading, enabling you to focus your attention on supporting your children as they develop the most important skills for reading:

- **Phonics** – decoding text (AF1) *(in Year 3)*
- **Literal comprehension** – literal understanding and retrieval from text (AF2)
- **Reading for meaning** – inference and prediction from text (AF3)
- **Appreciation** – understanding structure and purpose of text (AFs 4–7)

Full details indicating which AF is being assessed are shown in the mark schemes against every mark and analysed against sub-level in Appendix A.

Each test for each term has been carefully written to ensure there is a steady progression in the demand of both the reading pieces and the questions, as shown for Key Stage 2 in Table 1.1 (Table 4.3 on page 00 shows this progression across the *PiRA* series as a whole.)

The grids in Appendix A indicate the coverage and level of demand in finer detail, showing how the balance of demand shifts from the beginning of Year 3 through to the end of Year 6.

Table 1.1: Number of questions per NC sub-level in each *PiRA* test at Key Stage 2

	1c	1b	1a	2c	2b	2a	3c	3b	3a	4c	4b	4a	5c	5b	5a	Total
PiRA 3 Autumn		4	5	8	5	7	5	3	3							40
PiRA 3 Spring		2	4	7	3	4	8	8	2	2						40
PiRA 3 Summer		1	1	3	5	6	8	8	4	4						40
PiRA 4 Autumn			1	1	6	9	6	7	3	5	2					40
PiRA 4 Spring				1	5	3	9	6	6	4	4	2				40
PiRA 4 Summer					3	6	5	7	9	6	1	3				40
PiRA 5 Autumn						4	6	11	6	9	2	1	1			40
PiRA 5 Spring						2	2	7	10	7	6	3	3			40
PiRA 5 Summer						1	3	8	3	7	7	8	3			40
PiRA 6 Autumn							5	4	7	5	7	10	2			40
PiRA 6 Spring							2	7	3	10	11	4	1	2		40
PiRA 6 Summer							4	3	3	7	10	4	5	4		40

The autumn term tests are designed to be similar in demand to the previous summer term's test, to enable you to see if there has been any 'fall back' over the summer. A mark-for-mark 'raw score' comparison gives a helpful rule-of-thumb comparator to check, but reference to standardised scores and the *PiRA* Scale is more accurate.

PiRA — Administering the PiRA Tests

Giving the tests

When to test

The *PiRA* tests should ideally be used just before or shortly after the relevant half-term: they have been written to assess the teaching objectives from the second half of the previous term and first half of the current term along with earlier work, and are not dependent on what is taught in the second half of the current term.

This mirrors the original standardisation timings – in early November for autumn, late February for spring, and early May for summer – and will therefore give the most dependable data, but in practice using the tests one or two months either side of this 'optimum' point is unlikely to be critical.

Clearly, using the *PiRA* tests earlier rather than later in the second half of term can help the results to feed into and inform classroom practice.

How to test

Give each pupil a copy of the test booklet. Ask them to write their names on the front cover: the other information is best supplied by you or a teaching assistant when marking the test.

- Tell pupils that they will be reading a number of *short* stories, poems and non-fiction texts, and answering questions about them.
- In Year 4, 5 and 6 they should *gently* pull out the centre pages, as these form the reading booklet.
- Only in Year 3 do the questions follow the section of text: the questions are embedded in the stories and information, so that pupils will not be required to hunt through the text for answers. Also in Year 3 the first few questions on pages 2 and 3 may be read aloud, and you are advised to do this for the autumn test in particular. Everything else pupils should read for themselves.
- They should do their best to try to answer *all* the questions.
- Say that there will be some sections they can do easily, but that the test tends to get harder towards the end.
- They should not worry if they find some questions difficult, but just try their best and move on to see if they can answer some of the following questions.

Group size

You can administer the tests to whole classes or large groups if you feel comfortable doing so, but with Year 3 children it may be better with small groups supported by a teaching assistant. In the Year 3 trials, some teachers found it more effective to work with small groups – say five or six children of similar ability – so that a break could be taken if required. In Years 4 onwards, whole classes may be tested together unless a child is a very weak reader – then support from a teaching assistant may be helpful, working with an individual or with a small group of similar ability children.

Timing

A maximum time limit of **50 minutes** is set for the tests. In practice, in all years, the time is likely to be less than 40 minutes for most pupils, unless they are particularly slow readers or hesitant pupils.

Preparation

Each pupil will need the appropriate test booklet, and a pen or pencil. Answers may be altered by crossing or rubbing out.

Test conditions

If results are to be reliable, it is important that the pupils work alone, without copying or discussing their answers.

Administration

If any pupils are not clear about what they have to do, you may give additional explanation to help them to understand the requirements of the test, but do not read any of the actual questions, unless it is indicated they are to be mediated by a teacher or teaching assistant. Do not help with individual words.

Marking and recording results

Once the pupil has completed *PiRA*, their answers may be marked and, if required, analysed. A 'tick' line in the right-hand margin indicates where a mark might be awarded. Some questions have more than one part, or attract more than one mark, so you should follow the mark scheme carefully, using your professional judgement if necessary. For the resulting scores and levels to be valid, you should *not* award half-marks. (The code letter shown for each tick line is for use if you wish to profile the pupil's performance for closer investigation – see below.)

To assist marking and collating the data, there are boxes in which to record page totals at the bottom right of each appropriate page of the test booklets. Simply add up the ticks on a page, and write the page total in each box. (Note that the page totals correspond to the text type or genre, which is shown alongside the scores in the grid on the front cover.)

You can then transfer the page scores to the grid on the front of the test booklet, and total the column to find each pupil's total raw score (maximum 40 for each of the Key Stage 2 tests).

If you wish to profile the pupil's performance, total the number of correct answers the pupil has obtained in each coded category (i.e. **P** phonics, **L** literal comprehension, **M** reading for meaning, **A** appreciation of reading) and record these in the boxes in the bottom half of the grid on the front cover.

Refer to the appropriate tables in this manual to obtain the standardised score, reading age and NC level and sub-level for each pupil. You can then enter each pupil's scores on the photocopiable Record Sheet. Or use **PiRA Digital** to automate the whole score-conversion process and unlock *PiRA*'s performance analysis, diagnostic and predictive potential.

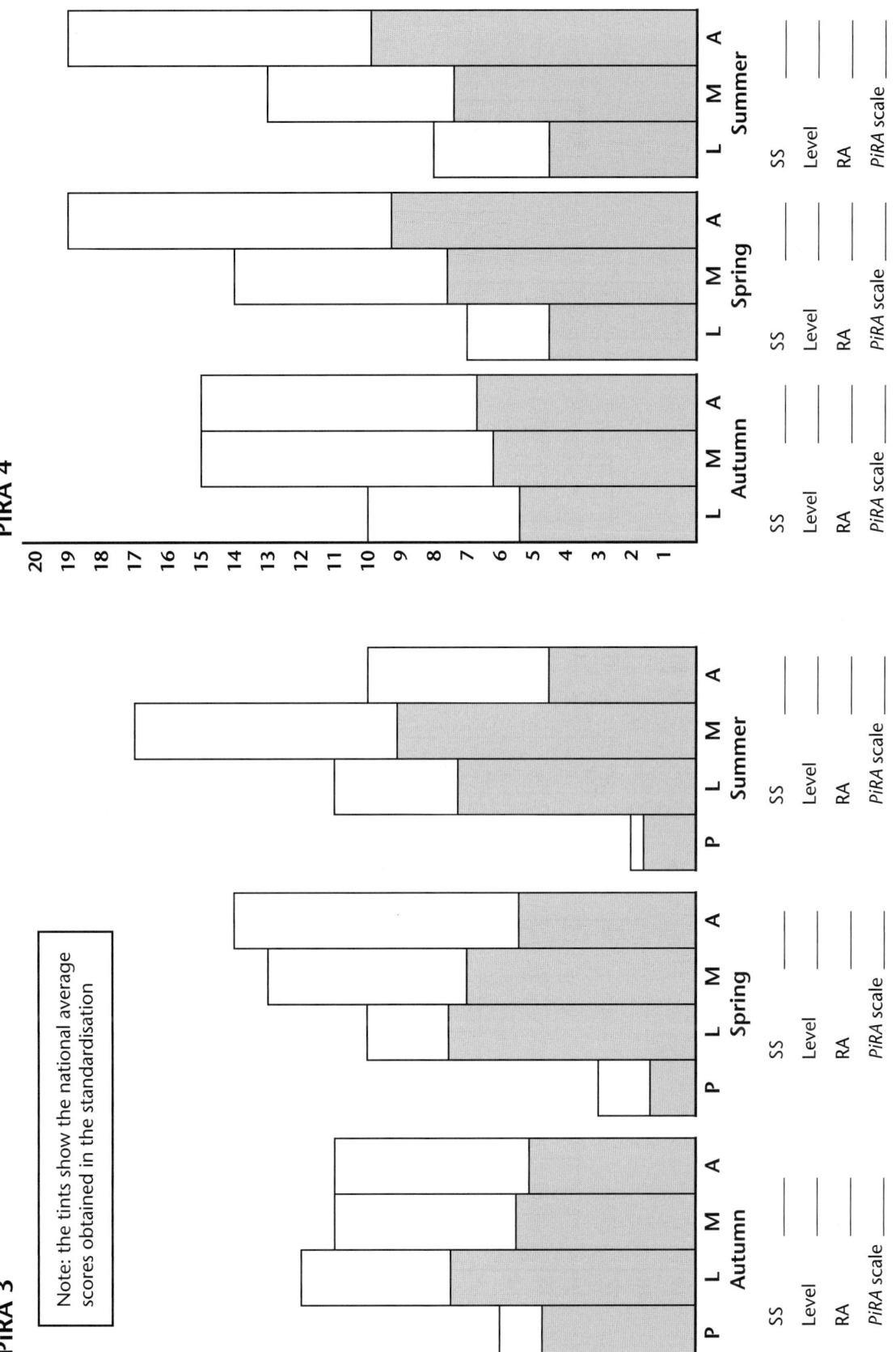

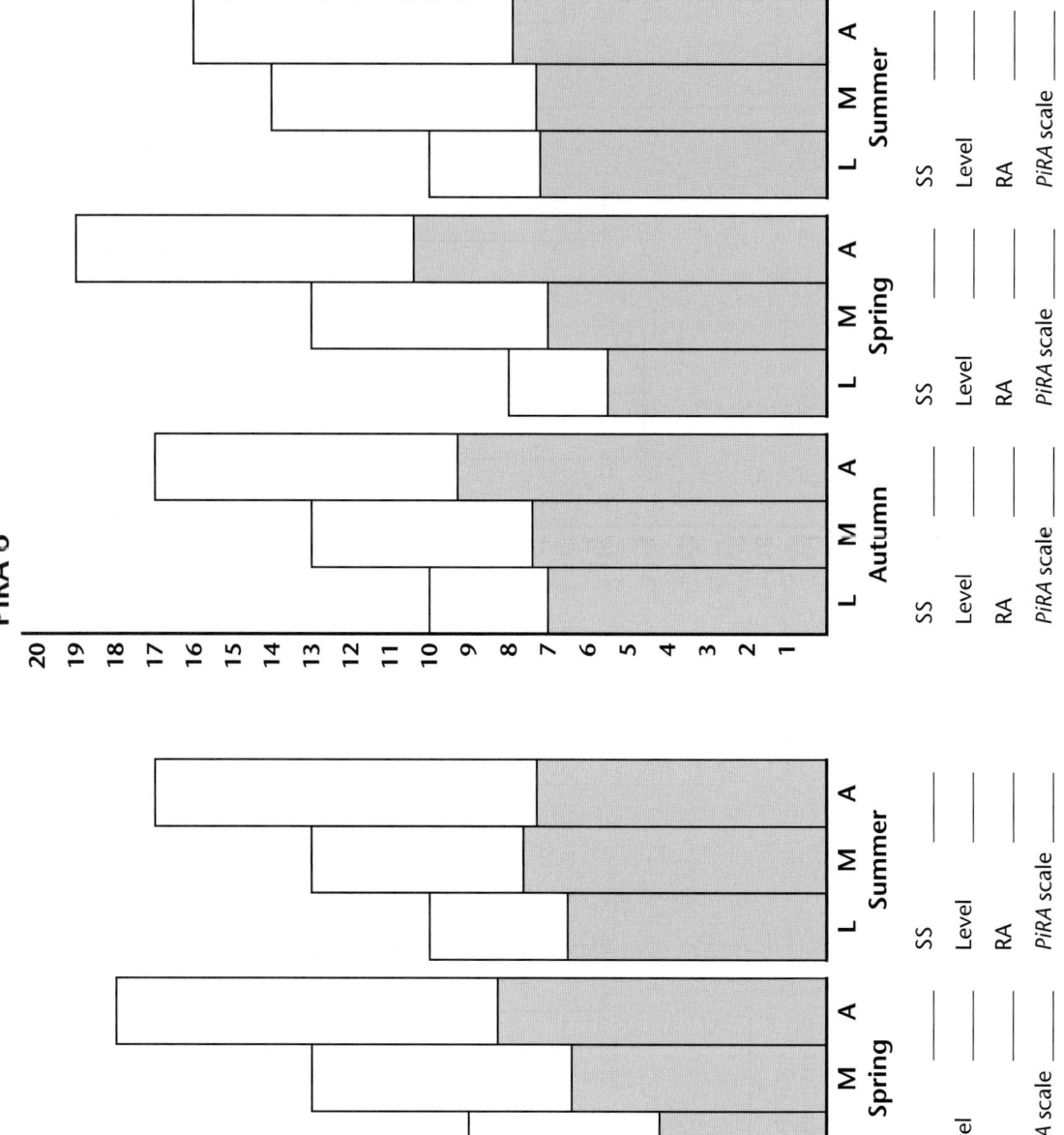

Obtaining and Interpreting Test Scores

The results obtained from *PiRA* will enable you to report pupil performance in terms of:

- age-standardised score;
- percentile (**Table 3.3**);
- reading age (**Table 3.4**);
- National Curriculum level, subdivided a, b or c (**Table 3.5**);
- APP level, subdivided as high, secure and low (**Table 3.5**);
- the *PiRA* Scale (**Table 3.5**).

Table 3.1 shows average scores for each year group, by gender, for each *PiRA* test as a whole, against which you can compare your own pupils' or class average raw scores.

Table 3.1: Average test marks (raw scores) by term and gender

	Autumn test			Spring test			Summer test		
	Boys	Girls	Total	Boys	Girls	Total	Boys	Girls	Total
PiRA 3	20.8	24.4	22.6	19.8	22.8	21.3	21.3	24.0	22.6
PiRA 4	17.0	19.4	18.0	20.2	22.5	21.3	20.7	22.6	21.6
PiRA 5	19.2	20.4	19.9	17.8	20.0	18.9	20.3	22.6	21.5
PiRA 6	23.0	24.2	23.5	21.9	24.1	23.0	21.4	23.5	22.5

Standardised scores and percentiles

There are a number of advantages of using age-standardised scores for comparing summative performance. These include:

- They are standardised to an average score of 100, immediately showing whether a pupil is above or below average, relative to *PiRA*'s national standardisation sample.
- They allow comparisons to take into account the pupils' ages: older pupils are likely to have higher *raw* scores than younger pupils, but could have a lower *standardised* score. This enables you to rank pupils in order of achievement after age has been accounted for. *Note:* with younger pupils, exposure to teaching is likely to have a significant if not a greater impact on achievement than the chronological age of the child.

Well-founded standardised scores can be averaged, to give an indication of the general attainment level of a class or even a whole intake: this is especially helpful when exploring school and teacher effectiveness, for it is unfair on schools and teachers to be judged as poor if they have a very weak intake yet can demonstrate their pupils are making good progress.

One disadvantage with age-standardised scores is that by their very nature they posit that older children will do better than younger children. In most tests, that span a number of years, this is indeed the case as age and experience does matter;

however, the *PiRA* tests are written for each individual year group and our research found that age correlated weakly with performance, particularly in the spring term tests. This is not surprising as the children were all receiving a fairly common experience based on national guidelines. This common experience tended to outweigh the effect of chronological age *per se*. Any differentiation in learning is not by age but by performance, so progress is likely to be, at best, weakly linked to age but much more reflective of innate ability of the child and quality of teaching, together with support and practice from school and home.

The **standardised scores** provided at the end of this manual range between 70 and 130, and the mean is 100. As can be seen from the normal distribution graph below, the six vertical bands determined by the standard deviation (SD) of 15 enable you to group pupils into:

- those whose performance is within an age-appropriate range (within one SD either side of the mean: i.e. 85–115);
- those who are below or above average in this regard (between one and two SDs either side of the mean: i.e. 70–85 and 115–130);
- those who are *well* below/*well* above the average for their age (between two and three SDs either side of the mean: i.e. below 70 or above 130);

For many teachers, the term *average*, based on 1 SD each side of the mean is too wide, and the *higher average* and *lower average* bands provide a finer set of descriptors.

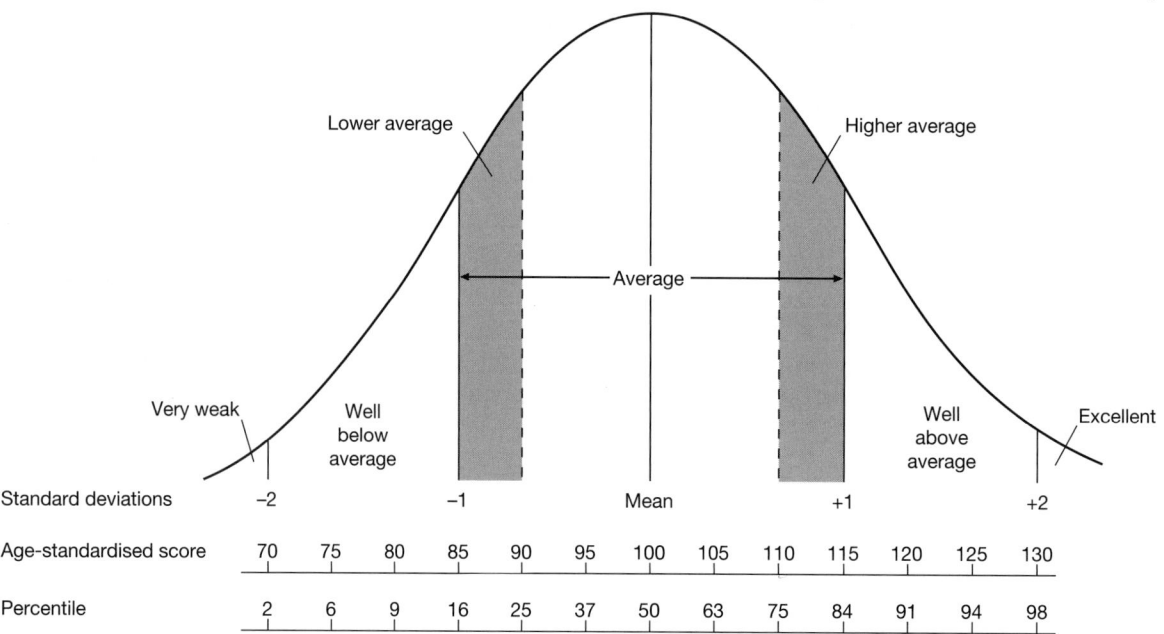

Table 3.2: Relationship between standardised test scores and qualitative interpretations

Standardised score	Qualitative interpretation of standardised scores	Standard deviation from mean	Percentile score	Percentage of normal population
>130	Excellent	>+2	>98	2.27
116–130	Well above average	+1 to +2	86–98	13.59
110–115 85–115 85–90	higher average Average/age-appropriate lower average	–1 to +1	16–84	68.26
70–84	Well below average	–1 to –2	2–14	13.59
<69	Very weak	<–2	<2	2.27

Obtaining and Interpreting Test Scores

A danger is that age-standardised scores can give a spurious accuracy and imply *too* fine a distinction – suggesting one pupil is better than another, where the confidence limit of the mark does not warrant this. Care is therefore advised and caution should be taken when placing pupils in order of merit.

The 90% confidence band for the Stage Two *PiRA* tests is typically plus or minus 4 (see Table 4.2) – so for a pupil with an age-standardised score of, say, 106 you can be 90% confident that their 'true' score is between 102 and 110.

Percentiles can help to give you a better feel for the significance of a pupil's reading age, because they show the percentage in each age group who score below a certain level. So a standardised score at the 68th percentile means that 68 per cent of the group scored below that pupil's standardised score. Thus the pupil is in the top third for his or her age group.

Percentile scores may be derived from standardised scores. To obtain a pupil's percentile, first calculate the pupil's chronological age and obtain his or her standardised score using the appropriate conversion table at the end of this manual, and then refer to Table 3.3.

The relationship between standardised scores and percentiles is most easily seen by reference to the normal distribution graph shown opposite.

Table 3.3: Relationship between standardised scores and percentiles

Standardised Score	Percentile	Standardised Score	Percentile	Standardised Score	Percentile
130+	98+	108	70	89	24
128–9	97	107	68	88	22
126–7	96	106	66	87	20
125	95	105	63	86	18
123–4	94	104	60	85	16
122	93	103	58	84	14
121	92	102	55	83	13
120	91	101	52	82	12
119	90	100	50	81	11
118	89	99	48	80	9
117	87	98	45	79	8
116	86	97	42	78	7
115	84	96	40	76–7	6
114	82	95	37	75	5
113	80	94	34	73–4	4
112	78	93	32	71–2	3
111	77	92	30	70	2
110	74	91	28	70–	1
109	72	90	26		

Reading ages and NC levels

Reading age is used by many teachers as a quick reference: a reading age shows the *average* chronological age of the pupils who obtained each particular raw score – i.e. the chronological age at which this level of performance is typical. As explained on pages 13–14, *PiRA* tests do not correlate closely with age. For more detailed comparative information, however, and especially for tracking progress over time, standardised scores and percentiles are to be preferred.

Note that *PiRA* reading ages are provided for ages beyond the normal age range for a given Year. These have been generated by using statistical extrapolations, by up to six months either side of the main range of Key Stage 2 pupils taking the tests in the trials. Such extrapolations can be especially useful in interpreting the performance of weaker readers who have been given a test for a younger age range.

National Curriculum and **APP levels** can be read off from Table 3.5 (pages 18–19).

Reporting progress: the *PiRA* Scale

Table 3.5 provides, for each test, a complete set of reference data for reporting progress in terms of NC and APP levels, points scores and a *PiRA* Scale score. It clearly illustrates the relationship we have established between NC and APP sub-levels. Whilst there is no officially published relationship, this is the commonly accepted pattern. Similarly, in the interests of providing finer details for teachers, we have filled in the even numbers in the points score column.

In developing the *PiRA* tests, seven cohorts of pupils – well over 10 000 pupils in all – were tracked termly over a full academic year. Using this information, plus the Optional and Key Stage test data, it was possible to link pupil performance from term to term and year to year, to identify patterns that provide a firm basis on which to project *future* performance and establish realistic expectations. The data was further strengthened by repeating the tests for Years 2 and 6 in successive summer terms, to gather an extra tier of year-on-year information with respect to Key Stages 1 and 2 and to provide a sample of over 1800 children across these two years. Table 3.7 draws this information together across all four years, from summer in Year 2 until summer Year 6.

The most useful 'level'-based monitoring scale is the *PiRA* Scale score, as it shows a decimalised level and gives an opportunity to monitor progress term-by-term at a much finer level than the a/b/c of NC sub-levels, APP levels or even the points scores used by many local authorities.

Table 3.4: Reading ages for each term

PiRA 3 mark	Autumn	Spring	Summer	PiRA 4 mark	Autumn	Spring	Summer	PiRA 5 mark	Autumn	Spring	Summer	PiRA 6 mark	Autumn	Spring	Summer
8				8				8				8			
9				9	<7:4			9	<8:5	<8:10		9			
10				10	7:4			10	8:6	8:10		10			
11				11	7:7			11	8:7	8:11		11			
12				12	7:9			12	8:9	9:1		12			
13				13	7:11			13	8:10	9:2		13			
14				14	8:2			14	9:0	9:4		14			
15				15	8:4			15	9:1	9:5	<9:2	15			
16				16	8:6			16	9:3	9:7	9:2	16			
17				17	8:8	<7:9	<8:2	17	9:5	9:8	9:5	17	<9:4		<10:3
18	<6:4	<6:10		18	8:11	7:9	8:2	18	9:6	9:10	9:7	18	9:5		10:3
19	6:5	6:10		19	9:1	8:0	8:5	19	9:8	9:11	9:9	19	9:7	<9:10	10:7
20	6:8	7:0	<7:1	20	9:3	8:4	8:8	20	9:9	10:0	9:11	20	9:10	9:10	10:11
21	6:10	7:3	7:1	21	9:6	8:7	8:11	21	9:11	10:2	10:1	21	10:0	10:1	11:3
22	7:1	7:6	7:5	22	9:8	8:10	9:2	22	10:0	10:3	10:4	22	10:3	10:4	10:11
23	7:3	7:9	7:8	23	9:10	9:2	9:5	23	10:2	10:5	10:6	23	10:5	10:7	11:3
24	7:6	8:0	8:0	24	10:0	9:5	9:7	24	10:3	10:6	10:10	24	10:8	10:11	11:7
25	7:8	8:2	8:4	25	>10:0	9:9	9:10	25	10:5	10:8	11:1	25	10:10	11:2	11:11
26	7:11	8:5	8:8	26		10:0	10:1	26	10:6	10:9	11:3	26	11:0	11:5	12:3
27	8:1	8:8	9:0	27		10:1	10:4	27	10:8	10:11	11:4	27	11:3	11:9	12:6
28	8:4	8:11	9:4	28		>10:1	>10:4	28	10:9	11:0	>11:4	28	11:5	12:0	>12:6
29	8:6	9:1	>9:4	29				29	10:11	11:1		29	11:8	12:2	
30	8:8	>9:1		30				30	11:0	>11:1		30	11:10	>12:2	
31	8:11			31				31	>11:0			31	12:0		
32	9:0			32				32				32	>12:0		
33	>9:0			33				33				33			
34				34				34				34			
35				35				35				35			

Obtaining and Interpreting Test Scores

Table 3.5: *PiRA* marks, scale scores and levels

First find the raw score in the column for the test your pupils have taken; then read across to obtain the 'level' information in the form you require.

Years 3 and 4

PiRA Scale	PiRA 3 Autumn marks	PiRA 3 Spring marks	PiRA 3 Summer marks	PiRA 4 Autumn marks	PiRA 4 Spring marks	PiRA 4 Summer marks	NC level	APP level	Points score	PiRA Scale
0.6	2–3						P7		7	0.6
0.7	4						P8		8	0.7
0.8	4						P8		8	0.8
0.9	5						P8		8	0.9
1.0	6		2				1c	1L	8	1.0
1.1	6		2				1c	1L	8	1.1
1.2	7		2				1c	1S	8	1.2
1.3	8	5	3			1	1b	1S	9	1.3
1.4	8	5	3			1	1b	1S	9	1.4
1.5	9	6	4			1	1b	1S	10	1.5
1.6	9	7	5	2		1	1b	1S	10	1.6
1.7	10	8	6	3	6	2	1a	1S	11	1.7
1.8	10	9	7	3	6	3	1a	1H	11	1.8
1.9	11	10	8	3	6	4	1a	1H	12	1.9
2.0	12	11–12	9	4	7	5	2c	2L	13	2.0
2.1	13–14	13–15	10–11	5	8	6	2c	2L	13	2.1
2.2	15–16	16–17	12–13	6–7	9	7–8	2c	2S	14	2.2
2.3	17–18	18	14	8–9	10	9	2b	2S	15	2.3
2.4	19–20	19	15	10–11	11	10	2b	2S	15	2.4
2.5	21–22	20	16	12	12	11	2b	2S	16	2.5
2.6	23–24	21–22	17–18	13	13	11	2b	2S	16	2.6
2.7	25–26	23	19	14	14	12	2a	2S	17	2.7
2.8	27–28	24–25	20	15	15	12	2a	2H	17	2.8
2.9	29–31	26–27	21–22	16–17	16–17	13	2a	2H	18	2.9
3.0	32–33	28	23	18–19	18	14	3c	3L	19	3.0
3.1	34–35	29	24	20	19–20	15	3c	3L	19	3.1
3.2	36	30	25–26	21	21–22	16–17	3c	3S	20	3.2
3.3	37	31	27	22	23	18	3b	3S	21	3.3
3.4	38	31	28	23	24	19	3b	3S	21	3.4
3.5	39	32	29	24	25	20	3b	3S	22	3.5
3.6	40	32	30	25	25	21	3b	3S	22	3.6
3.7		33	31	26	26	22	3a	3S	23	3.7
3.8		34	32	27	27	23	3a	3H	23	3.8
3.9		35	33	28	28–29	24–25	3a	3H	24	3.9
4.0		36	34	29	30	26	4c	4L	25	4.0
4.1		37–38	35	30	31	27	4c	4L	25	4.1
4.2		39–40	35	31	31	28	4c	4S	26	4.2
4.3			36	32	32	29	4b	4S	27	4.3
4.4			37	33	32	30	4b	4S	27	4.4
4.5			38	33	32	31	4b	4S	28	4.5
4.6			39	34	32	32	4b	4S	28	4.6
4.7			40	35–36	33–35	33	4a	4S	29	4.7
4.8				37–38	36–38	34	4a	4H	29	4.8
4.9				39–40	39–40	35–36	4a	4H	30	4.9
5.0						37–40	5c	5L	31	5.0

Obtaining and Interpreting Test Scores

Years 5 and 6

PiRA Scale	PiRA 5 Autumn marks	PiRA 5 Spring marks	PiRA 5 Summer marks	PiRA 6 Autumn marks	PiRA 6 Spring marks	PiRA 6 Summer marks	NC level	APP level	Points score	PiRA Scale
1.5							1b	1S	10	1.5
1.6							1b	1S	10	1.6
1.8		4	2				1a	1H	11	1.8
1.9		4	3				1a	1H	12	1.9
2.0	2	5	4	3		2	2c	2L	13	2.0
2.1	3	5	5	4		3	2c	2L	13	2.1
2.2	4	5	5	5		4	2c	2S	14	2.2
2.3	5	6	6	6	5	5	2b	2S	15	2.3
2.4	6–7	6	6	7	5	6	2b	2S	15	2.4
2.5	8	6	7	8	6	6	2b	2S	16	2.5
2.6	9	6	7	9	6	6	2b	2S	16	2.6
2.7	10	7	8	10–11	7	7	2a	2S	17	2.7
2.8	10	8	9	12	7	8	2a	2H	17	2.8
2.9	11	9–10	10	13	8	9	2a	2H	18	2.9
3.0	12	11	11	14	9	10	3c	3L	19	3.0
3.1	13–14	12	12	14	10–11	10	3c	3L	19	3.1
3.2	15	12	12	15	12–13	10	3c	3S	20	3.2
3.3	16	13	13	16	14	11	3b	3S	21	3.3
3.4	17	14	14	17	14	12	3b	3S	21	3.4
3.5	18	15	15	17	14	12	3b	3S	22	3.5
3.6	19	15	15	18	14	12	3b	3S	22	3.6
3.7	20	16	16	19	15	13	3a	3S	23	3.7
3.8	21–22	17	17	20	16–17	14	3a	3H	23	3.8
3.9	23	18–19	18	20	18–19	14	3a	3H	24	3.9
4.0	24	20	19	21–22	20	15	4c	4L	25	4.0
4.1	25	21–22	20	23	21	16–17	4c	4L	25	4.1
4.2	26	23	21–22	24	22	18	4c	4S	26	4.2
4.3	27	24	23	25	23	19	4b	4S	27	4.3
4.4	28	25	24	26	24	19	4b	4S	27	4.4
4.5	29	26	25	27	25	20	4b	4S	28	4.5
4.6	30	27	26	28	25	21	4b	4S	28	4.6
4.7	31	28	27	29	26	22	4a	4S	29	4.7
4.8	32–33	29	28	30	27	23	4a	4H	29	4.8
4.9	34	30–31	29	31	28	24	4a	4H	30	4.9
5.0	35	32	30	32	29	25–26	5c	5L	31	5.0
5.1	36	33	31	33–34	30	27–28	5c	5L	31	5.1
5.2	37–38	33	32–33	35	31	29–30	5c	5S	32	5.2
5.3	39–40	34–35	34	36	32	31	5b	5S	33	5.3
5.4		36–37	35	37	33	32	5b	5S	33	5.4
5.5		38–39	36	38	33	33	5b	5S	34	5.5
5.6		40	37	39	34	34-35	5b	5S	34	5.6
5.7			38–40	40	35–36	36–37	5a	5S	35	5.7
5.8					37–38	38–39	5a	5H	35	5.8
5.9					39–40	40	5a	5H	36	5.9

Obtaining and Interpreting Test Scores

Predicting future performance

The tests for each term have been designed to provide questions covering a range of demand appropriate to the year and term (see Appendix A and Table 1.1). Table 3.7 allows you to see at a glance the *PiRA* Scale score of a pupil in any one term, and to track immediately to the column next right to see the anticipated *PiRA* Scale score they will obtain if they make average progress. As the tests have been designed to challenge the pupils around the level at which they are expected to be working, you may well find that pupils get similar *raw scores* from term to term within each Year, but their level of performance, as shown in the *PiRA* Scale score, will of course be continuing to increase.

You may wish to set targets for the future and monitor progress over a term or year. This is possible for both individual pupils and whole classes, by reference to the average performance data of over 1000 pupils in each year group, from term to term and across all the years, in the standardisation sample. Tables 3.7–3.8 provide this information.

In Key Stage 2, expected progress is usually at least one NC sub-level every other term. Some children do better than this, others less well. Table 3.7 shows how, on average, pupils gaining different *PiRA* Scale scores move on in subsequent terms up the *PiRA* Scale. Look up the term in which the pupil took the test and follow across to see the anticipated *PiRA* Scale score they should achieve if they follow the progress of an average pupil.

So, for example. a pupil who starts Key Stage 2 having got a *PiRA* Scale score of 16 (equivalent to NC level 2b) on the *PiRA* Year 2 summer test, and who makes average progress, might be expected to have a *PiRA* Scale score of 3.0 (level 3c) and a mark of 23 in the Year 3 summer test, and 3.8 (level 3a) and a mark of 23 in the Year 4 summer test – and ultimately to gain a 5b in Year 6 with a *PiRA* prediction of 5.3 and a mark of around 32. In practice, of course, no one pupil is 'average' and progress is rarely completely smooth. And the further ahead one is looking, the more tentative are the predictions one can make (see also below). But the *PiRA* Scale does provide a well-founded statistical basis for making predictions about performance which can then be modified in the light of actual progress.

Thus, should a pupil do *better* than anticipated in a subsequent term, move down the row you are reading across to reflect their improved performance. Similarly if a pupil does *not* reach the anticipated average score for the next term, then move up to find the *PiRA* Scale score that they have achieved and read across to see the revised prediction if they now do make average progress.

Monitoring the difference between the **actual** *PiRA* Scale score and the **predicted** average *PiRA* Scale score – for an individual pupil or for a whole class – enables you to see if there is increasing divergence or convergence to normal progress.

Obviously, for each term that a pupil is away from the original base mark or 'score', the more tenuous is the link. This linking is weakest where we move from summer term in one year to autumn term in the next year. However, we are able to use what is known as common anchor equating to link through summer-based levels (derived from TA or key stage or optional tests) from the summer *PiRA* score to the following term's autumn *PiRA* score.

Table 3.8 provides a cross-check opportunity to monitor average progress from the beginning of a year (i.e. autumn) to the end of year (i.e. summer), in effect skipping the spring data, for Years 3 to 6. This may be helpful to gain a snapshot of a pupil's (or class') likely performance at the end of a school year. The information in Table 3.8 was obtained via a separate set of equatings to that given in Table 3.7. The results are very similar, but not identical.

Table 3.7a: Monitoring and predicting progress from term to term, from summer Year 2 through Years 3 and 4

Average PiRA 2 Summer *PiRA* Scale score	Average PiRA 3 Autumn *PiRA* Scale score	Average PiRA 3 Spring *PiRA* Scale score	Average PiRA 3 Summer *PiRA* Scale score	Average PiRA 4 Autumn *PiRA* Scale score	Average PiRA 4 Spring *PiRA* Scale score	Average PiRA 4 Summer *PiRA* Scale score
						1.9
						2.0
						2.1
						2.0
				1.4	1.7–1.8	2.3
				1.5	1.9	2.3
				1.6	2.0	2.4
				1.7–1.9	2.1	2.5–2.6
				2.0	2.2	2.7
			2.0	2.1	2.3	2.8
	0.6	1.3–1.4	2.1	2.2	2.4	2.9
0.5	0.6	1.5	2.1	2.2	2.5	3.0
0.6	0.7–0.8	1.6	2.2	2.3	2.5	3.0
0.7	0.8–0.9	1.6	2.2	2.3	2.6	3.1
0.8–0.9	1.0–1.1	1.7	2.2	2.3	2.6	3.1
1.0	1.2	1.8	2.3	2.4	2.7	3.2
1.1	1.3–1.4	1.9	2.4	2.4	2.8	3.2
1.2	1.5–1.6	1.9	2.4	2.5	2.9	3.3
1.3–1.6	1.7–1.8	2.0	2.5	2.5	2.9	3.3
1.7–1.9	1.9	2.0	2.5	2.6	2.9	3.3
2.0	2.0	2.1	2.6	2.7	2.9	3.3
2.0	2.1	2.1	2.6	2.8	3.0	3.4
2.1	2.2	2.1	2.7	2.9	3.1	3.5–3.6
2.2	2.2	2.2	2.8	2.9	3.1	3.5–3.6
2.2	2.3	2.2	2.8	2.9	3.1	3.5–3.6
2.4	2.4	2.4	2.9	3.0	3.2	3.7
2.5	2.5	2.5	3.0	3.1	3.2	3.8
2.5	2.6	2.6	3.1	3.2	3.3	3.8
2.6	2.7	2.7	3.2	3.3	3.4	3.9
2.6	2.7	2.7	3.2	3.4	3.5–3.6	3.9
2.7	2.8	2.8	3.3	3.5	3.7	4.0
2.8	2.9	2.9	3.4	3.6	3.8	4.1
2.9	3.0	3.0	3.5	3.7	3.8	4.1
3.0	3.0	3.1	3.6	3.8	3.9	4.2
3.0	3.0	3.1	3.6	3.9	3.9	4.2
3.1	3.1	3.2	3.7	4.0	4.0	4.3
	3.2	3.3	3.8	4.1	4.1–4.2	4.4
			3.9	4.2	4.3–4.4	4.5
			4.0	4.3	4.5–4.6	4.6
				4.4–4.5	4.7	4.7
				4.6	4.7	4.7
				4.7	4.7	4.7
				4.7	4.8	4.8
				4.8	4.8	4.9
				4.9	4.9	5.0

Obtaining and Interpreting Test Scores

Table 3.7b: Monitoring and predicting progress from term to term, from summer Year 4 through Years 5 and 6

Average PiRA 4 Summer *PiRA* Scale score	Average PiRA 5 Autumn *PiRA* Scale score	Average PiRA 5 Spring *PiRA* Scale score	Average PiRA 5 Summer *PiRA* Scale score	Average PiRA 6 Autumn *PiRA* Scale score	Average PiRA 6 Spring *PiRA* Scale score	Average PiRA 6 Summer *PiRA* Scale score
				2.1	2.3–2.4	3.3
				2.2	2.5–2.6	3.4–3.6
			1.8	2.3	2.7–2.8	3.7–3.8
			1.9	2.4	2.9	3.9
			2.0–2.2	2.5	3.0	3.9
			2.3–2.4	2.6	3.0	3.9
			2.5–2.6	2.7	3.1	4.0
			2.7	2.8	3.2	4.1
		1.8	2.8	2.9	3.3	4.2
		1.9	2.9	3.0–3.1	3.4–3.6	4.3
1.9	2.0	2.0	3.0	3.2	3.7	4.4
2.0	2.1	2.2	3.1	3.3	3.8	4.5
2.1	2.2	2.3	3.2	3.4–3.5	3.8	4.5
2.2	2.3	2.4	3.2	3.6	3.9	4.6
2.2	2.4	2.5–2.6	3.3	3.7	3.9	4.7
2.3	2.4	2.7	3.4	3.8–3.9	4.0	4.8
2.4	2.5	2.8	3.5–3.6	4.0	4.0	4.8
2.5–2.6	2.6	2.9	3.7	4.0	4.1	4.9
2.7–2.8	2.7–2.8	2.9	3.8	4.1	4.2	4.9
2.9	2.9	3.0	3.8	4.2	4.3	5.0
3.0	3.0	3.1–3.2	3.9	4.3	4.4	5.0
3.1	3.1	3.3	4.0	4.4	4.5	5.1
3.2	3.2	3.4	4.1	4.5	4.6	5.1
3.3	3.3	3.5–3.6	4.2	4.6	4.7	5.1
3.4	3.4	3.7	4.2	4.7	4.8	5.1
3.5	3.5	3.8	4.2	4.8	4.9	5.2
3.6	3.6	3.9	4.3	4.9	5.0	5.2
3.7	3.7	3.9	4.4	5.0	5.1	5.3
3.8	3.8	4.0	4.5	5.1	5.2	5.3
3.9	3.9	4.1	4.6	5.1	5.3	5.4
4.0	4.0	4.1	4.6	5.2	5.4	5.5
4.1	4.1	4.2	4.7	5.3	5.4	5.5
4.2	4.2	4.3	4.8	5.4	5.5	5.6
4.3	4.3	4.4	4.9	5.5	5.6	5.6
4.4	4.4	4.5	5.0	5.6	5.6	5.6
4.5	4.5	4.6	5.1	5.7	5.7	5.7
4.6	4.6	4.7	5.2	5.7	5.7	5.8
4.7	4.7	4.8	5.2	5.7	5.8	5.8+
4.8	4.8	4.8	5.2			
4.9	4.9	4.9	5.3			
5.0	5.0	5.0	5.4			
5.0	5.1	5.1–5.2	5.5			
	5.2	5.3	5.6			
	5.3	5.4	5.7			
		5.4	5.7			
		5.5	5.7			
		5.5	5.7			

Table 3.8: Monitoring and predicting progress from autumn to summer within each Year

Year 3		Year 4	
Average PiRA 3 Autumn *PiRA* Scale score	Average PiRA 3 Summer *PiRA* Scale score	Average PiRA 4 Autumn *PiRA* Scale score	Average PiRA 4 Summer *PiRA* Scale score
0.6	2.1	1.6	2.2
0.7–0.8	2.1	1.7–1.9	2.3
0.9	2.2	2.0	2.4
1.0–1.1	2.2	2.1	2.4
1.2	2.2	2.2	2.5–2.6
1.3–1.4	2.3	2.2	2.7–2.8
1.5–1.6	2.4	2.3	2.9
1.7–1.8	2.5	2.4	3.0
1.9	2.5	2.4	3.1
2.0	2.6	2.5	3.2
2.1	2.6	2.6	3.2
2.1	2.7	2.7	3.2
2.2	2.8	2.8	3.3
2.3	2.9	2.9	3.4
2.4	3.0	2.9	3.5
2.5	3.1	3.0	3.5
2.5	3.2	3.0	3.6
2.6	3.2	3.1	3.7
2.6	3.3	3.2	3.8
2.7	3.3	3.3	3.8
2.7	3.4	3.4	3.9
2.8	3.5	3.5	3.9
2.8	3.6	3.6	4.0
2.9	3.6	3.7	4.1
2.9	3.7	3.8	4.1
2.9	3.8	3.9	4.2
3.0	3.9	4.0	4.3
3.0	4.0	4.1	4.4
3.1	4.1	4.2	4.4
3.1	4.2	4.3	4.5
3.2	4.3	4.4–4.5	4.6
3.3	4.4	4.6	4.7
3.4	4.5	4.7	4.7
3.5	4.6	4.7	4.8
		4.8	4.9
		4.9	5.0

Obtaining and Interpreting Test Scores

Year 5   Year 6

Average PiRA 5 Autumn PiRA Scale score	Average PiRA 5 Summer PiRA Scale score	Average PiRA 6 Autumn PiRA Scale score	Average PiRA 6 Summer PiRA Scale score
	2.7	2.0	2.9
2	2.8	2.1	2.9
2.1	2.9	2.2	3.0–3.2
2.2	3.0	2.3	3.3
2.3	3.1	2.4	3.3
2.4	3.2	2.5	3.4–3.6
2.4	3.3	2.6	3.7
2.5	3.4	2.7	3.8
2.6	3.5	2.7	3.9
2.7–2.8	3.6	2.8	4.0
2.9	3.7	2.9	4.1
3	3.8	3–3.1	4.1
3.1	3.9	3.2	4.1
3.1	4.0	3.3	4.2
3.2	4.0	3.4–3.5	4.3
3.3	4.1	3.6	4.4
3.4	4.2	3.7	4.5
3.5	4.2	3.8–3.9	4.6
3.6	4.2	4.0	4.7
3.7	4.3	4.0	4.8
3.8	4.4	4.1	4.8
3.8	4.5	4.2	4.9
3.9	4.6	4.3	5.0
4.0	4.6	4.4	5.0
4.1	4.7	4.5	5.0
4.2	4.8	4.6	5.1
4.3	4.9	4.7	5.1
4.4	4.9	4.8	5.2
4.5	5.0	4.9	5.2
4.6	5.1	5.0	5.2
4.7	5.2	5.1	5.3
4.8	5.2	5.1	5.4
4.9	5.3	5.2	5.4
5.0	5.4	5.3	5.5
5.1	5.5	5.4	5.6
5.2	5.5	5.5	5.6
5.2	5.6	5.6	5.7
5.3	5.7	5.7	5.8

Obtaining and Interpreting Test Scores

Diagnostic and formative interpretation

Summative measures are valuable, but only give an *overall* picture of the young person's performance relative to his/her peers. Such data may, for example, confirm that the pupil is doing well for his/her age and indicate that no intervention strategy is required. However, a more detailed check may show, for example, that good literal reading accuracy is masking a weakness in comprehension and inference.

1. **Use the Profile to see if there are patterns of strengths and weaknesses in:**
   Phonics – decoding and extracting meaning of text (Year 3 only)
   Literal comprehension – literal understanding and retrieval from text
   Reading for meaning – inference and prediction from text
   Appreciation of reading – understanding structure and purpose of text

Every pupil has particular strengths and weaknesses that will show up in the *PiRA* profile. When you examine the pupil's answers, you can see when there is a change from correct to incorrect, and at what level of demand this is occurring. This may alert you to generally weak achievement or perhaps to weakness (or strength) in one specific aspect of reading. This may highlight aspects of literacy which have previously been taught but which have been forgotten or were not understood at the time.

It should be borne in mind when undertaking this form of analysis that performance will naturally reflect recent teaching.

2. **You may also go one stage further and check a pupil's individual performance on a specific question** and compare how they have performed relative to other pupils in the same year group. Refer to Appendix B (at the end of this manual) to see what proportion of pupils in that year group answered each question correctly. This is called the facility and is shown as a percentage: 60% shows that 60% of pupils in the national sample answered the question correctly.

The case studies on pages 26–9 indicate how this comparative information enables some next steps to be planned. With this more detailed picture, it is possible to implement specific teaching strategies to help weak and even good readers to improve.

The *PiRA* tests may be taken as pencil-and-paper exercises or as **PiRA Digital** on-screen, at a computer. The latter is the more effective way to pinpoint strengths and areas of weakness, as it marks and analyses the patterns of performance automatically – at total score, Profile score and even individual-question levels.

For pupils taking the pencil-and paper tests, **PiRA Digital** gives you the option of entering *total* raw scores or – for more detailed analysis – the mark *for each of the three or four Profile strands*. The latter is obviously more time-consuming, but rewards you with a complete record, held electronically, and a useful set of performance analyses. It also allows you to track pupil performance term-by-term as they progress from phonics to reading for meaning and appreciation of reading.

Whether you input your data by total raw score or by Profile scores from the front cover of the test paper, **PiRA Digital** provides predictions of future performance and allows you to look back to see if present progress is as would have been expected.

Three case studies

Katlyn

Katlyn's history is helpful to us in Year 3. An August-born child, she had done quite well in Year 1 and had finished the year with a *PiRA* Scale score of 1.1 and a standardised score of 95, which was very slightly below average for her age. She began Year 2 well, scoring 11 in the Year 2 autumn *PiRA* – the equivalent of 1.5 on the *PiRA* scale and a standardised score of 101. But in the spring term, she fell back to a standardised score of 97. Although this decline was trivial, it corroborated the class teacher's concern that Katlyn seemed to be losing confidence, so the teacher asked the literacy coordinator to investigate further.

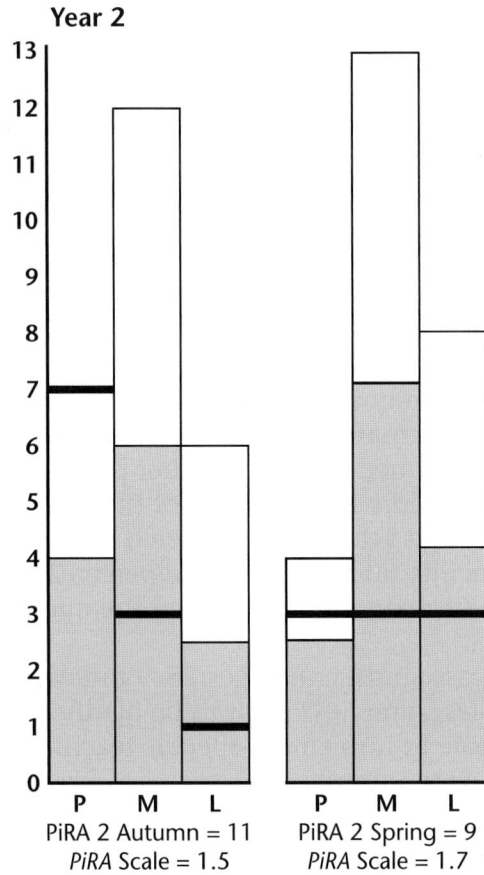

The literacy coordinator's report referenced the mark schemes in the *PiRA* manual, because they showed the levels of the individual questions. This showed that Katlyn was getting all of the level 1 questions correct, but hardly any of the level 2.

Therefore, the strategy agreed for the summer term of Year 2 was to:

- move Katlyn into a higher literacy group and to ask another child to be a literacy buddy and response partner. We recognised that Katlyn needed additional support to access new ideas, but didn't want her to become dependent on a teaching assistant. This higher group works less on decoding and more on responding to texts;

- change her reading scheme so that we could move her onto harder books without signalling that fact to her;

- talk to her Mum to ask her to let Katlyn read to herself rather than reading aloud, but then to talk about the book together.

The summer term results – 12 marks in total (P 4, L 5, M 3), or a *PiRA* Scale score of 2.3 – were much more encouraging. Katlyn was now much more confident as a reader and was showing close to the expected average progress over Year 2. She should be well prepared for her move into Key Stage 2.

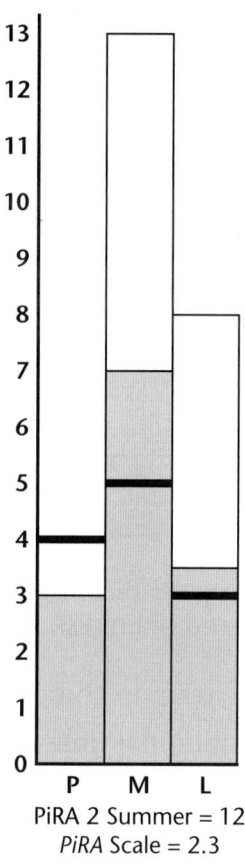

PiRA 2 Summer = 12
PiRA Scale = 2.3

It is good to see how Year 2 had addressed some things that would in the longer run have caused us problems in Year 3. The average scores for the national sample, as well as the maximum scores, profile Katlyn's strengths and weaknesses very well and provide a good baseline for us to use to work with her. (*Her Profile analysis would have been so much easier if we'd done the test electronically – but the bar-chart Record Sheet displays it well*).

Samir

Samir started Key Stage 2 working within level 3 in some subjects, but his reading and writing did not match his verbal skills. In summer of Year 3 we assessed him using the Year 2 *PiRA* summer test, as he could not cope with the summer Year 3 *PiRA* test. We found he had made little or no progress from Key Stage 1 – we actually wondered if he was moving backwards! In Year 4 we used the Year 2 autumn and spring tests rather than Year 3 or Year 4 *PiRA* tests, to ensure he could engage with the reading texts and had the questions on the same page as the reading material. These results confirmed his continued lack of progress in Year 4. (We made the judgement to continue to use the Year 2 tests based on the fact that our teacher assessment for reading was 2b. Level 2b fell around the middle of the range of marks available in that test, as shown in the table on page 9 of the *PiRA* Stage One manual.) At a pupil progress interview, at the end of the spring term in Year 4, he was identified as a cause for concern.

I undertook an analysis of his three sets of Year 2 *PiRA* results (shown below). They show that he was not gaining any of the marks for Reading for Meaning (**M**, AF3). That surprised us: although he is an EAL child, he has been in school since the beginning of Year 2 and his spoken English is very colloquial – he even speaks with a local accent! We know that his writing level is low – but it always has been and he is a very reluctant writer.

	Test used	Phonics – Samir's mark	Phonics – Max possible (national average)	Literal Comprehension – Samir's mark	Literal Comprehension – Max possible (national average)	Reading for Meaning – Samir's mark	Reading for Meaning – Max possible (national average)	Samir's total (max 25)	PiRA Scale score
Summer Year 3	PiRA 2 Summer	4	4 (2.9)	8	13 (7.7)	1	8 (4.1)	13	2.4
Autumn Year 4	PiRA 2 Autumn	6	7 (4.2)	9	12 (5.9)	1	6 (2.4)	16	2.0
Spring Year 4	PiRA 2 Spring	4	4 (2.6)	8	13 (7.1)	2	8 (4.2)	14	2.1

At the pupil progress meeting, we started to think more about the possibility that Samir's command of English may not be as good as it seems. Our strategy was to:

- ask the EAL team to come and do a detailed analysis of Samir's English;
- give him additional time with our EAL Teaching Assistant, with the specific intention of looking at idioms;
- use the ideas for advanced learners in the EAL toolkit (http://nationalstrategies.standards.dcsf.gov.uk/node/85322)
- use opportunities in ICT to explore his written sentence construction. *Clicker 5* (Crick software) allows us to use word banks and jumbled sentences, so we can see whether he can construct a complex sentence;
- introduce a small-group speaking and listening programme to focus on reasoning and explanations;
- use opportunities in guided reading to explore his use of inference.

The EAL analysis showed that Samir did indeed have weaknesses in his understanding of more advanced and subtle English. We were able to target the interventions to address those very explicitly. Our anecdotal evidence was that, almost week by week, Samir's confidence in answering inferential questions grew. His access to the rest of the curriculum also improved – as did his willingness to write. We were pleased, then, that the summer term *PiRA* results were more encouraging – a significantly improved Reading for Meaning score (7), and an overall 22 marks out of 40 giving a *PiRA* Scale score of 2.9 – although there is still more work to do. The *PiRA* tests were useful in helping us to pick up this problem – we should have done so earlier and are reviewing our use of the *PiRA* analyses for all children in all years.

Mia

Our school has found that the official Optional tests for reading have not given us accurate or useful information, so we have always used teacher assessment rather than test information to track pupil progress. We used *PiRA* for the first time this year.

When Mia began Year 6, we had high expectations of her reading – she was predicted a level 5. But when she sat the *PiRA* autumn test in October, she scored only 16, a level 3b. We were confident that the *PiRA* tests were sound, as other children did as expected. Since most of her other short tests and AfL work matched teacher assessment, we recognised that we needed to look more carefully at Mia's reading.

Immediately, we saw the problem: Mia hadn't answered most of the questions. We did an analysis of the questions she *had* answered and matched these to the facilities tables in the back of the manual. This offered us two hypotheses: either she stopped working when she was faced by a harder question, or she was an unusually slow reader.

We decided that the best way forward was to sit with Mia while she did the Year 5 autumn test in order to observe her test technique. It became immediately clear that she read quite slowly, but that this was compounded by the fact that she started re-reading the text from the beginning as she answered each question.

The way forward was clear: we taught her techniques and strategies for answering comprehension questions. The effectiveness of this strategy was proved in the spring term, when she scored 22 marks (a *PiRA* Scale score of 4.2 – a top level 4c, and just in a 4S for APP). This puts her on track for a level 4a with this considerable increase in performance – or with her newly acquired test answering skills, she might even get a level 5.

PiRA
Technical Information

Trialling and standardisation

Overall, 46 schools took part in the *PiRA* tests trials. The government school performance website showed that, in the Key Stage 2 national tests for 2008, those schools participating in the trials had 80.9% of their pupils gaining a level 4 or above (of whom 28.5% gained a level 5).

The government statistics showed that, in 2008, 81% of pupils nationally achieved level 4 or above, and in 2009, 79% achieved level 4 or above. Overall, therefore, the *PiRA* schools' performance is very closely representative of primary schools across the country. The schools also reflected a wide cross-section in terms of school size and location and the language mix of the pupils, as shown in Table 4.1.

Table 4.1: Description of schools in the trials, including home languages of pupils

Language mix of pupils	Demography of school			
	Central large town/city	Suburban large town/city	Small town	Village
Only English as home language	–	2	3	5
Fewer than 5 different home languages	2	5	3	10
Between 6 and 19 different home languages	3	6	1	–
More than 20 home languages	3	3	–	–
Totals	8	16	7	15

In total, 10 846 pupils took part in the standardisation trials, although through absence when tests were taken, and as a result of moving schools and the like, the core cohort that provided the 'all-through' term-on-term links was between 7500 and 8000 pupils – that is, over 1000 per year group, except in the Reception year where it was 850 in the trials. (A number of Early Years teachers did not wish to use a formal test with the very youngest children.) Table 4.2 provides fuller information about the pupils making up the sample.

Reliability

The *reliability* of a test indicates whether or not we would get similar results from repeated administrations of the test with similar samples of pupils. An appropriate measure of test reliability for *PiRA* is Cronbach's Alpha (α), which measures internal consistency reliability. A value above 0.60 is considered the minimum acceptable for most forms of educational assessment. This information for each test is given in Table 4.2 and shows that the tests are extremely reliable.

Test theory tells us that test reliability is also related to test length, and suggests that any test should comprise 25 or more marks to achieve reasonable reliability.

For tests targeting a particular age range, we use a standardisation method based on *percentile norms* – the fundamental principle being that scores at the same percentile rank are comparable. Hence a pupil at, say, the 30th percentile in his/her age group has the same relative ability as a pupil at the 30th percentile in any other age group. The standardisation procedure that we have used for these tests is called the *non-parallel linear regression model*. It is the recognised method for standardising educational tests.

Any scores derived from a short test are subject to some margin of error. This does not mean that a child has been assessed incorrectly, but rather that we are making a statistical estimate of the accuracy of the test as a measuring instrument. There are two ways of reporting the margin of error. One is the standard error of measurement ('SE measurement' in Table 4.2), the other is the 90% confidence band.

The 90% confidence bands are calculated during the fitting of linear regression lines to the P5, P10 … P90, P95 isopercentiles during the age standardisation process. The confidence bands are not the same measure as the standard error of measurement shown in the item analysis report which is calculated directly from pupils' raw test data.

The 90% confidence band for the Stage Two *PiRA* age standardised scores is +/- 4. This means, for example, that for a child aged say 9:2 (nine years and two months) who obtains a raw score of 18 marks on the autumn Year 4 test and hence a standardised score of 98, we can say with 90% confidence that their 'true' standardised score lies between 94 and 102. Table 4.2 gives the reliability data for each of the tests.

In Table 4.2, the 'Pearson Coefficient' is a measure of the correlation between pupils' *PiRA* raw scores and either their national test scores or their teacher-assessed levels as supplied by schools. A perfect match would be 1. The fact that these are higher in the summer term reflects the fact that this is when NC levels are 'officially' reported, as well as the teachers' longer familiarity with their pupils and their individual attainments (see also Appendix C).

Validity

Strong *face validity* of a test is the test designer's shorthand for saying the test addresses the material in the curriculum which the children have studied and been taught. Each test in the *PiRA* series of twenty tests from Reception to Year 6 has been written to follow the national guidelines for the second half of the previous term and the first half of the term the test is set for. This ensures these tests, which should ideally be taken soon after half term each term, meet the *validity* criterion.

The *validity* of the age standardisation is improved if there is good correlation between pupils' test scores and age. Additionally, the test itself must have high reliability (see above) so that the results would be replicated by repeated administrations of the test. Children who were in Year 2 and Year 6 took the same summer *PiRA* tests in subsequent years showed very similar performance (see Table 4.2 for the Year 6 data).

Table 4.2: Sample statistics and reliability measures

	Autumn	Spring	Summer 2010	Summer 2009
PiRA 3				
Sample size	1215	1205	1123	
Boys	612	590	559	
Girls	603	615	563	
Mean	22.6	21.3	22.6	
SE measurement	2.48	2.50	2.56	
Cronbach alpha	0.94	0.93	0.91	
Pearson Coefficient	0.78	0.77	0.79	
90% confidence band about the mean	22.2–23.2	20.9–21.8	22.2–23.0	
PiRA 4				
Sample size	1251	1249	1120	
Boys	653	655	583	
Girls	598	594	537	
Mean	18.0	21.3	21.6	
SE measurement	2.62	2.60	2.26	
Cronbach alpha	0.92	0.93	0.92	
Pearson Coefficient	0.74	0.77	0.78	
90% confidence band about the mean	17.7–18.6	20.9–21.8	21.2–22.0	
PiRA 5				
Sample size	1197	1158	1056	
Boys	586	569	516	
Girls	611	589	540	
Mean	19.9	18.9	21.5	
SE measurement	2.73	2.60	2.63	
Cronbach alpha	0.91	0.93	0.90	
Pearson Coefficient	0.76	0.76	0.78	
90% confidence band about the mean	19.4–20.3	18.5–19.4	21.1–21.9	
PiRA 6				
Sample size	1255	1217	1109	731
Boys	633	607	553	362
Girls	622	610	556	369
Mean	23.5	23.0	22.2	22.9
SE measurement	2.68	2.59	2.64	2.64
Cronbach alpha	0.89	0.92	0.91	0.89
Pearson Coefficient	0.77	0.74	0.64	0.72
90% confidence band about the mean	23.2–24.0	22.6–23.4	21.8–22.6	22.5–23.3

To ensure validity, we also compared the *PiRA* tests with the current (2006) Optional tests for Years 3, 4 and 5 and the 2009 KS1 and KS2 national tests, applying the same standards criteria to confirm that *PiRA* tests are of similar demand in terms of coverage of sub-levels. These results are shown at the foot of Table 4.3. In comparison with the national tests, the *PiRA* tests contain less text material and less referencing to specific individual paragraphs, but more emphasis on reading for meaning, as recommended in *Letters and Sounds* once phonics have been established.

Table 4.3: *PiRA* tests and NC tests analysed for range of demand

PiRA test:	P6	P7	P8	1c	1b	1a	2c	2b	2a	3c	3b	3a	4c	4b	4a	5c	5b	5a	Total
R Spring	5	4	9	5	2														25
R Summer	3	3	5	6	7	1													25
Y1 Autumn	1	2	2	6	9	3	2												25
Y1 Spring		3	1	5	8	4	2	2											25
Y1 Summer		1	1	1	5	9	5	3											25
Y2 Autumn		1	1	3	3	7	5	4	1										25
Y2 Spring			2	1	1	4	8	5	2	1	1								25
Y2 Summer				1	3	3	6	5	3	2	2								25
Y3 Autumn				4	5	8	5	7	5	3	3								40
Y3 Spring				2	4	7	3	4	8	8	2	2							40
Y3 Summer				1	1	3	5	6	8	8	4	4							40
Y4 Autumn					1	1	6	9	6	7	3	5	2						40
Y4 Spring						1	5	3	9	6	6	4	4	2					40
Y4 Summer							3	6	5	7	9	6	1	3					40
Y5 Autumn								4	6	11	6	9	2	1	1				40
Y5 Spring								2	2	7	10	7	6	3	3				40
Y5 Summer								1	3	8	3	7	7	8	3				40
Y6 Autumn									5	4	7	5	7	10	2				40
Y6 Spring									2	7	3	10	11	4	1	2			40
Y6 Summer									4	3	3	7	10	4	5	4			40
	P6	P7	P8	1c	1b	1a	2c	2b	2a	3c	3b	3a	4c	4b	4a	5c	5b	5a	Total
2009 KS1 L2					2	7	5	6	6	2									28
2009 KS1 L3							1	5	6	5	4	5							26
Y3 Optional					1	3	3	7	8	5	3	5	1						36
Y4 Optional							6	7	6	7	8	6	4						44
Y5 Optional						1	3	5	8	8	7	7	1	3	3	2			48
2009 KS2								2	5	6	6	7	9	5	1	7	2		50

Gender differences

In all years and terms, girls out-perform boys. This is consistent with national patterns of reading tests and English tests in general.

Table 4.4: Average marks (raw scores) for each of the *PiRA* tests, showing gender differences

Average raw scores for each year in the Autumn tests

	PiRA 1	PiRA 2	PiRA 3	PiRA 4	PiRA 5	PiRA 6
Mean score	13.2	12.6	22.6	18.0	19.9	23.5
Avg boys	12.3	11.9	20.8	17.0	19.2	23.0
Avg girls	14.8	13.0	24.4	19.4	20.4	24.2
Max. score	25	25	40	40	40	40

Average raw scores for each year in the Spring tests

	PiRA R	PiRA 1	PiRA 2	PiRA 3	PiRA 4	PiRA 5	PiRA 6
Mean score	13.3	11.1	13.8	21.3	21.3	18.9	23.0
Avg boys	13.0	10.9	13.4	19.8	20.2	17.8	21.9
Avg girls	13.7	11.4	14.2	22.8	22.5	20.0	24.1
Max. score	25	25	25	40	40	40	40

Average raw scores for each year in the Summer tests

	PiRA R	PiRA 1	PiRA 2	PiRA 3	PiRA 4	PiRA 5	PiRA 6
Mean score	15.9	13.6	14.7	22.6	21.6	21.5	22.5
Avg boys	15.6	13.2	14.0	21.3	20.7	20.3	21.4
Avg girls	16.3	14.2	15.4	24.0	22.6	22.6	23.5
Max. score	25	25	25	40	40	40	40

 Answers & Mark Schemes: PiRA 3

Please use professional judgement when marking, recognising that children often write more words than the brief, crisp answers given in the mark scheme.
Capital letters are not required unless specifically stated in the mark scheme.
Do not penalise spelling: as long as the meaning is clear, always award the mark.
Where a question asks for, say, 3 answers ticked and a pupil ticks 4, deduct one mark.

PiRA 3 Autumn

	KEEPING PETS	Mark	Level	Profile (AF)
1	cow	1	1b	P (AF1)
2	2 marks if three or four animals are correctly matched; 1 mark for one or two correct.	1 1	1b 1a	P (AF1)
3	Any one from: Rabbits, hamsters and guinea pigs Cats and kittens Dogs and puppies *Initial capital letter not necessary for the mark.*	1	2a	A (AF4)
4	KEEPING PETS *Accept words in lower case.*	1	2a	A (AF4)
5	to show what each part of the text is about	1	2c	A (AF4)
6	cats *(do not accept kitten)*	1	2a	L (AF2)
7	rabbit — faithful pet hamster — lives outside dog — sleeps during day *All required for the mark.*	1	3c	L (AF2)
8	scratch	1	1a	L (AF2)
9	She thinks some animals make good pets.	1	2b	M (AF3)
10	Any two from: headings and sub-headings pictures introduction	1	2b	A (AF7)
11(a)	a dog *(accept dogs)*	1	2b	L (AF2)
11(b)	yes or no or any comment relating to the answer to 11(a).	1	2c	A (AF6)
12	A cat is a　　　　loving　　pet. A dog is a faithful but expensive pet. *Both required for the mark.*	1	3c	A (AF5)
13	a farm *or* farms *Do not accept field or outside.*	1	2c	L (AF2)
	total	15		
	Billy's Tooth			
14	Billy's tooth *(accept Billy's loose tooth)* *Apostrophe and capital letter not required.*	1	1b	L (AF2)
15	loose *(accept wobbly)*	1	1a	L (AF2)
16(a)	Billy *(capital letter required)*	1	2c	L (AF2)

PiRA 3 mark schemes　35

16(b)	tooth Accept teeth or mouth; do not accept face.	1	2c	P (AF1)	
17	My tooth is loose. These four and no other words should be circled.	1	2a	A (AF4)	
18	Billy's teacher	1	2b	M (AF3)	
19	heads (accept head)	1	1a	L (AF2)	
20	Jason	1	2c	L (AF2)	
21	Any one from: fell out came out was knocked out he lost it	1	3c	M (AF3)	
22	his tooth	1	3c	M (AF3)	
23	He wanted to show how hard they crashed.	1	2a	A (AF5)	
24	Creeping or creeping up (no other words circled)	1	2b	A (AF5)	
25	They wanted to help. They wanted to see what was happening.	1 1	3b 3b	M (AF3)	
26	Billy	1	3c	M (AF3)	
27	Because Mrs Williams is fed up with Billy talking about his tooth.	1	3b	A (AF4)	
28	3. Jason was creeping up on Billy. 1. Billy was 'It'. 4. Billy and Jason crashed. 2. Billy sat behind a bush to get his breath back. Award 2 marks for all four correct; 1 mark for any two correct.	1 1	3a 3a	M (AF3) M (AF3)	
	total	18			
	Mum				
29	Mum	1	1b	L (AF2)	
30	glum chum	1 1	1a 2c	P (AF1) P (AF1)	
31	feed it or give it food	1	2c	L (AF2)	
32	pause	1	3a	A (AF4)	
33	makes things that were wrong alright again makes us feel better when we're hurt	1 1	2a 2a	M (AF3) M (AF3)	
	total	7			
	Overall	40			

PiRA 3 Autumn: analysis

Pages and text type	Questions	Max mark	National average mark
2–5, non-fiction	1–13	15	9.3
6–9, story	14–28	18	9.8
10–11, poem	29–33	7	3.6
PiRA Profile			
Phonics		6	4.7
Literal comprehension		12	7.5
Reading for meaning		11	5.5
Appreciation of reading		11	5.1
Total		40	**22.6**

PiRA 3 Spring

Family Snapshot

		Mark	Level	Profile (AF)
1(a)	Family Snapshot	1	1b	A (AF4)
1(b)	Anna	1	1b	A (AF4)
2	Pappy (accept Grandpa)	1	2c	L (AF2)
3	Joan – moan Bert – hurt Both required for the mark.	1	2c	P (AF1)
4	because it was a family birthday party.	1	2a	M (AF3)
5	No	1	3c	A (AF6)
6	Jill (accept mother or mum, do not accept sister) Pappy (accept Grandpa) Dad (accept Blake or father) Anna (accept 'me' or 'The writer') 1 mark for three or four correct.	1	2a	M (AF3)
7	Daisy – lazy: Yes ✓ Jane – complain: Yes ✓ does – fuzz: Yes ✓ Here – there: No ✓ All required for the mark.	1	2b	P (AF1)
	total	8		

A Present for Dad

		Mark	Level	Profile (AF)
8	three or 3	1	1a	L (AF2)
9	a mint	1	2c	L (AF2)
10	one – coins two – hairgrips three – buttons four – mint All required for the mark.	1	2c	L (AF2)
11	Dad and Jo Both required for the mark.	1	1a	L (AF2)
12	Zack	1	2c	L (AF2)
13	robot, baby doll, mini-skateboard, red ball 1 mark for three or four correct.	1	3c	L (AF2)
14	play with	1	2c	L (AF2)
15	"I'd like that robot please," said Zack. "How much is it?" 1 mark if both parts of speech circled; No marks if 'said Zack' is also included.	1	3a	A (AF4)
16	a kitten	1	3c	M (AF3)
17	unwilling	1	3b	M (AF3)
18	to make you read it clearly	1	3c	A (AF5)
19	favourite toys	1	2c	L (AF2)
20	Jo knows what to get.	1	3c	A (AF4)
21	Free Accept 'Kittens' also ringed as well as Free.	1	2a	A (AF5)
22	what she could give Dad	1	3b	M (AF3)
23	Jo getting a present for her dad	1	3b	M (AF3)
	total	16		

	Quad Roller Skates			
24	plate and boot correctly labelled *Both required for the mark.*	1	2b	P (AF1)
25	quad roller skates	1	1a	M (AF3)
26	four *or* 4	1	1a	L (AF2)
27	metal strap-on skate	1	3c	M (AF3)
28	Later *or* nowadays *Accept* still	1	3c	A (AF4)
29	speed quad — plastic plate with wheels roller dance skate — trainer with plate and wheels plastic strap-on skate — boot with plate and wheels *1 mark for two or three correct.*	1	3b	M (AF3)
30	so they don't get hurt if they fall	1	2b	M (AF3)
31	take a tumble *All three words – and no others – must be ringed for the mark.*	1	2a	A (AF5)
32	needed	1	3b	A (AF5)
33	Tells you what the text under it is about — label A picture to show you what the text is about — diagram Tells you what something in a picture is called — heading bullet points	1 1 1	3b 3b 3b	A (AF4) A (AF4) A (AF4)
34	to give information about quads	1	3c	M (AF3)
35	People should keep safe when they skate. People should have fun when they skate.	1 1	4c 4c	M (AF3) M (AF3)
36	Parts of a quad: — six main parts of a quad Different types of quad: — wise skaters wear helmets Protective gear: — speed quads are becoming more popular *1 mark for two or three correct.*	1	3a	A (AF4)
	total	16		
	Overall	40		

PiRA 3 Spring: analysis

Pages and text type	Questions	Max mark	National average mark
2–3, poem	1-7	8	4.8
4–7, story	8-23	16	9.6
8–11, non-fiction	24-36	16	6.8
PiRA Profile			
Phonics		3	1.4
Literal comprehension		10	7.6
Reading for meaning		13	7.0
Appreciation of reading		14	5.4
	Total	40	21.3

PiRA 3 Summer

	Bees	Mark	Level	Profile (AF)
1	Words joined correctly to bee and flower *Both required for the mark.*	1	1b	P (AF1)
2	spring	1	1a	L (AF2)
3	The queen finds a warm dark space — to make a nest. The queen makes a bed of pollen — to lay her eggs on. The queen makes a honey pot — to drink from. *All required for the mark.*	1	3c	L (AF2)
4	Two or 2	1	2c	L (AF2)
5	new queen → lays different eggs / hatches in late summer old queen → finds a place to sleep until next spring / dies in late summer *2 marks if three or four lines correct;* *1 mark if one or two lines correct.*	1 1	3b 3b	M (AF3) M (AF3)
6	1 egg, 4 bee, 3 cocoon, 2 grub *All required for the mark.*	1	3b	L (AF2)
7	All correctly labelled for the mark.	1	2b	P (AF1)
8	queen bees — drink honey from wax pots grubs — eat pollen beds worker bees — bite open cocoons	1 1 1	3c 3c 3c	L (AF2) L (AF2) L (AF2)
9	It is mostly facts.	1	3b	A (AF6)
	total	12		

	The Bike Ride			
10	Any two from: new (*accept* brand new), red *and/or* present	1	2c	A (AF5)
11	Bedroom or room (*Do not accept* house *or* home)	1	2c	L (AF2)
12(a)	in the past few days	1	3b	M (AF3)
12(b)	(Callum had) only been out on it once. **only** and **once** must be underlined for the mark to be awarded.	1	3c	M (AF3)
13	limped	1	2b	M (AF3)
14	his bike a horse *Both required for the mark.*	1	2b	L (AF2)
15	collapsed	1	3a	A (AF5)
16	Callum phones home	1	3c	M (AF3)
17	doing his homework — bored riding his bike — excited sitting on the grass — worried *All required for the mark.*	1	3a	M (AF3)
18	4 Callum went flying through the air. 2 Callum was standing up on the pedals. 3 Callum's front wheel hit a stone. 1 Callum was feeling good about his bike ride. *All required for the mark.*	1	3b	A (AF4)
19	Callum	1	2a	M (AF3)

20	change of place change of time change of action *All three required for the mark.*	1	4c	A (AF4)
21	He'll be angry.	1	3c	M (AF3)
22(a)	It was warm and sunny.	1	2a	M (AF3)
22(b)	blue sky and fluffy white clouds. *(all required for the mark)*	1	2a	L (AF2)
	total	15		

	Three Billy Goats Gruff			
23	playscript	1	2a	A (AF7)
24	under the bridge *Accept* at *or* by *the bridge, but not* on *the bridge*	1	2b	L (AF2)
25	sweet *and* green *Both required for the mark.*	1	2b	A (AF5)
26	he wants to encourage Little Billy to cross the bridge. he knows that Little Billy likes eating grass. *Both required for the mark.*	1	4c	M (AF3)
27	scared	1	2a	M (AF3)
28	So you will stress the word, saying it louder.	1	3b	A (AF4)
29	Little Billy	1	2a	M (AF3)
30	admiring worried	1 1	3a	M (AF3)
31	so the actor doesn't speak the word aloud so the actor knows what to do as well as what to say *Both required for the mark.*	1	3c	A (AF4)
32		Little	Middle	Big			
	Not enough grass left			✓	1	4c	M (AF3)
	Afraid of being eaten by the Troll	✓	✓		1	4c	M (AF3)
	In the lower box, both ticks required for the mark.						
33	cunning	1	3b	A (AF6)
	total	13		
	Overall	40		

PiRA 3 Summer: analysis

Pages and text type	Questions	Max mark	National average mark
2–4, non-fiction	1–9	12	8.2
5–8, story	10–22	15	8.8
9–12, playscript	23–33	13	5.7
PiRA Profile			
Phonics		2	1.6
Literal comprehension		11	7.3
Reading for meaning		17	9.1
Appreciation of reading		10	4.5
	Total	40	22.6

PiRA Answers & Mark Schemes: PiRA 4

Please use professional judgement when marking, recognising that children often write more words than the brief, crisp answers given in the mark scheme.
Capital letters are not required unless specifically stated in the mark scheme.
Do not penalise spelling: as long as the meaning is clear, always award the mark.
Where a question asks for, say, 3 answers ticked and a pupil ticks 4, deduct one mark.

PiRA 4 Autumn

	Another Start	Mark	Level	Profile (AF)
1	Lisa *(accept Lisa and her mum)*	1	1a	L (AF2)
2	in a school *or* the head's office	1	2a	M (AF3)
3	five	1	2a	L (AF2)
4	She was trying not to cry.	1	3c	M (AF3)
5	smiled bravely *Both words required for the mark.*	1	3b	M (AF3)
6(a)	reading books *(accept books or colour)*	1	2a	L (AF2)
6(b)	she loved reading *or* likes books	1	2a	L (AF2)
7		Old schools	New school				
	Smell of sweaty feet	✓				
	New carpet		✓	1	3c	L (AF2)
	Bored children at school	✓				
	All required for the mark.					
8(a)	No	1	2c	M (AF3)
8(b)	bad smell	1	3b	M (AF3)
	dirty	1	3b	M (AF3)
9	He smiled *Accept He asks if she is ready.*	1	3c	M (AF3)
10	She had taken a long time to get to sleep.	1	2a	M (AF3)
11	Lisa moved to the best flat. 2 Badly behaved children disrupted Lisa's learning. 1 Lisa met her new headteacher. 3 *All required for the mark.*	1	3a	M (AF3)
12	real-life story	1	3c	A (AF7)
	total	15		

	A Day in the Life of Roger Hunter			
13	Kirsty Pippins *(accept Kirsty)* *Do not accept the interviewer or presenter or her name*	1	2a	A (AF4)
14	playscript	1	3c	A (AF7)
15	to tell us how this author spends his days	1	3c	A (AF6)
16	*Any one from:* to show who's talking or speaking to show that two people are talking because it's a playscript *Do not accept they are initials*	1	3a	A (AF4)
17	Rule	1	2a	A (AF5)

18	research stage — no hours a day writing stage — 12 hours a day handed to publisher — 5–6 hours a day plus evenings (research stage → 5–6 hours a day plus evenings; writing stage → 12 hours a day; handed to publisher → no hours a day) *2 marks for three correct;* *1 mark for one or two correct.*	1 1	3b 3a	L (AF2) M (AF3)
19	Interviewer *(accept* presenter*)*	1	2a	M (AF3)
20	how he spends his time	1	2b	L (AF2)
21	My brain needs a bit of time to recover → I am very tired By the time the story is fully grown → When the story is finished It's very intense → I work very hard It's the most exciting and scary story I've written → I want you to buy my book. (also: I want you to know that) *2 marks for three or four correct;* *1 mark for one or two correct.*	1 1	4c 4c	M (AF3) M (AF3)
22	Some of the words are in *italics* → They are titles, which are important to the text. Some of the words are in **bold** type → They give information about the people. Kirsty Pippin and Roger Hunter have capital letters → They are names of people. *2 marks for three correct;* *1 mark for one or two correct.*	1 1	3b 3b	A (AF4) A (AF4)
23	squirrel's acorn store *(accept* acorn*)*	1	4c	A (AF5)
24	adventure fiction	1	3b	A (AF7)
	total	15		
Time				
25	eyes skies sighs	1 1 1	2b 2b 2b	A (AF5) A (AF5) A (AF5)
26	*Any one from:* *Time*'s a bird and Time just flies *Time* just flies *Accept* trying to catch him.	1	2a	L (AF2)
27	a jockey a thief	1 1	2b 2b	L (AF2) L (AF2)
28	*Any one from:* She wants to show that Time is very important in the poem. She's using the word Time as a name.	1	4b	A (AF4)
29	footprints	1	4b	A (AF5)
30	the moon	1	4c	M (AF3)
31	sad *Accept* 'with tears and sighs'	1	4c	M (AF3)
	total	10		
	Overall	40		

PiRA 4 Autumn: analysis

Pages and text type	Questions	Max mark	National average mark
2–4, story	1–12	15	7.6
5–7, interview	13–24	15	6.9
8, poem	25–31	10	3.7
PiRA Profile			
Literal comprehension		10	5.4
Reading for meaning		15	6.2
Appreciation of reading		15	6.7
	Total	40	18.0

PiRA 4 Spring

	Survival Foods				Mark	Level	Profile (AF)
1	grasshoppers ants *Both required for the mark.*				1	2b	L (AF2)
2	under logs; in old nests *Both required for the mark.*				1	2b	L (AF2)
3	So that you know what not to eat.				1	3c	A (AF6)
4	*Any two from:* insects that sting brightly coloured insects hairy insects insects that smell bad *Both required for the mark.*				1	2a	L (AF2)
5	You need to know which plants you can eat.				1	3a	A (AF6)
6		T	F	DNS	1	3b	M (AF3)
	All plants are safe to eat.		✓				
	You can eat any berry.		✓		1	3c	L (AF2)
	Plants are green.			✓	1	3b	M (AF3)
7	*Heading: any one from:* Survival Foods Thank Goodness there's Goodness in Bugs Plants: Poison or Pudding *Label:* grub				1 1	3c 3c	A (AF4) A (AF4)
8	To separate important points of information.				1	4c	A (AF4)
9	Thank Goodness ...Bugs! exclamation Plants: Pudding or Poison alliteration				1 1	3c 3a	A (AF5) A (AF5)
10		Fact	Opinion				
	Some mushrooms can be poisonous.	✓					
	Insects can taste better if you cook them.		✓		1	4c	M (AF3)
	It can be fun finding plants and bugs to eat to survive.		✓				
	All required for the mark.						
				total	14		

	Marooned	Mark	Level	Profile (AF)
11	delighted	1	2b	M (AF3)
12	bath (*accept* warm bath) carpet (*accept* luxury carpet)	1 1	3c 3c	M (AF3) M (AF3)
13	passion fruit — plump pineapples — prickly mangoes — blushing *All required for the mark.*	1	2a	L (AF2)
14	plunged headlong into the water. *Accept* swim *or* went swimming *or* dived.	1	3a	L (AF2)
15	He wants you to feel what it was like to be there.	1	3b	A (AF5)
16(a)	But what was that? *Ignore any further words written after the sentence.*	1	3a	A (AF4)
16(b)	He heard a noise.	1	3b	M (AF3)
17	In the first part – relaxed In the second – scared	1 1	4b 4b	M (AF3) M (AF3)
18	to send a message for help	1	3b	M (AF3)

19	itchy sand — second part sun scorching my neck — first part dappled sunlight — second part golden sand felt wonderful — second part chased by bears — first part *All required for the mark.*		1	4c	A (AF4)
20	*Any one from:* desperately Frantically *Do not accept* thankfully.		1	4c	A (AF6)
21	The writing reflects the writer's panic.		1	4a	A (AF5)
22	It frightened the writer. It sounded like an angry noise. It was a screeching sound. *All required for the mark.*		1	3b	M (AF3)
23	adventure story		1	3a	A (AF7)
		total	16		

Attic Fanatic

24	rats *and* alligators *Both required for the mark.*	1	2c	L (AF2)
25	scaly *(do not accept 'furry')*	1	3c	A (AF5)
26	get rid of them	1	3c	M (AF3)
27	ceiling – feeling	1	2b	A (AF5)
	things – wings	1	2b	A (AF5)
28	dad	1	4a	M (AF3)
29	imagine	1	3a	M (AF3)
30	scared	1	2a	A (AF6)

31		Verse 1	Verse 2	Not in either			
	What the poet hears in bed.	✓					
	Which creatures might be in the attic.		✓		1	4b	A (AF7)
	What the things in the attic are doing.	✓			1	4b	A (AF7)
	What dad says he will do.			✓			
	2 marks for four correct; *1 mark for two or three correct.*						

		total	10		
		Overall	40		

PiRA 4 Spring: analysis

Pages and text type	Questions	Max mark	National average mark
2–3, non-fiction	1–10	14	8.3
4–6, story	11–23	16	8.2
7–8, poem	24–31	10	4.8
PiRA Profile			
Literal comprehension		7	4.5
Reading for meaning		14	7.6
Appreciation of reading		19	9.3
	Total	40	21.3

PiRA 4 Summer

	Parkside Pupils Playground Protest	Mark	Level	Profile (AF)
1	school *or* primary school *Do not accept just* Primary.	1	2b	M (AF3)
2	*Any one from* He likes or plays football He represents football He's captain *Accept* he is a goalkeeper.	1	2a	M (AF3)
3	Jill Twitter — Pupil Sarah — Parent David Brown — Headteacher Jim Parkinson — Chair of Governors *All required for the mark.*	1	3b	L (AF2)
4	*Any one from:* storms argues states suggests comments	1	3b	A (AF5)
5	*Any three from:* recycle paper walk to school bike to school turn off lights make food for the birds/feed the birds *(Do not accept 'do all sorts of stuff'.)*	1 1 1	2a 2a 2a	L (AF2) L (AF2) L (AF2)
6		No	Yes				
	Pupils	✓		1	4c	M (AF3)
	Parents	✓				
	Governors		✓			
	All required for the mark.					
7	alliteration	1	3a	A (AF5)
8	the effect of new classrooms being built	1	2b	M (AF3)
9	the pupils and parents	1	4a	A (AF6)
10(a)	in a newspaper	1	2a	A (AF7)
10(b)	There is a headline. It reports different people's opinions. *Both required for the mark.*	1	3b	A (AF4)
	total	13		

	At The Airport			
11	America *or* USA *Accept* To see his Dad *or* Dad's wedding	1	2a	L (AF2)
12	*Any one from:* Airports are so boring Jim sighed again. He wished he was at home.	1	3c	M (AF3)
13	An air hostess *Do not accept* babysitter.	1	3b	M (AF3)
14	gobbling	1	3c	A (AF5)
15	Jim — looking at planes Jim — going to America Sandy — bored Sandy — reading 1 mark for correct three lines from Jim; 1 mark for correct two lines from Sandy.	1 1	4c 4c	L (AF2) L (AF2)

46 PiRA 4 mark schemes

16	Suddenly *(capital letter not required)*	1	3a	A (AF4)
17(a)	Any two from: scruffy crumpled dirty green *Both required for the mark.*	1	3c	A (AF5)
17(b)	They make the writing more interesting. They help to build up a picture in your head. *Both required for the mark.*	1	3b	A (AF6)
18(a)	rabbit	1	3c	L (AF2)
18(b)	scanning the landscape scenting danger *Both required for the mark.*	1	3a	A (AF5)
19	Any two from: darted, creeping *or* inching *Both required for the mark.* *Do not accept* crouched *or* heading *or* hiding.	1	3a	A (AF5)
20	feels sorry for him	1	4c	A (AF6)
21	The story is about Jim and his feelings.	1	4a	A (AF6)
22	Jim — freedom Sandy — work the young man — boredom (Jim–boredom, Sandy–work, the young man–freedom) *All required for the mark.*	1	3b	M (AF3)
	total	15		

Whose Turn?

23	They're on a school trip	1	2b	M (AF3)
24	*jumping down*	1	3b	A (AF4)
25	new line for each new speaker no speech marks instructions in brackets	1 1 1	3a 3a 3a	A (AF7) A (AF7) A (AF7)
26	five *or* 5	1	3c	M (AF3)
27	unkind *and* cunning *Both required for the mark.*	1	4b	M (AF3)
28	2 Ryan and his friends get off the climbing frame 4 Break ends 1 Helen asks Ryan why they are on the climbing frame 3 Mrs Lake talks to Ryan and his friends *All required for the mark.*	1	3a	A (AF4)
29	to Sam — who the character is talking to a few seconds later — time is passing politely — how something is said pointing — what the character is doing *All required for the mark.*	1	3a	A (AF4)
30			T	F	DNS
Ryan had been thinking about the climbing frame before break.	✓		
Ryan is being kind to the Year Threes.		✓	
Mrs Lake is easily fooled.		✓	| *2 marks for three correct;* *1 mark for one or two correct.*	1 1	4c 4c	M (AF3) M (AF3)
31	He thought he was being clever. He was the leader of his group of friends during this playtime. *Both required for the mark.*	1	4a	M (AF3)
	total	12		
	Overall	40		

PiRA 4 mark schemes 47

PiRA 4 Summer: analysis

Pages and text type	Questions	Max mark	National average mark
2–3, report	1–10	13	8.0
4–6, story	11–22	15	8.0
7–8, playscript	23–31	12	5.5
PiRA Profile			
Literal comprehension		8	4.5
Reading for meaning		13	7.4
Appreciation of reading		19	9.9
	Total	40	21.6

PiRA Answers & Mark Schemes: PiRA 5

Please use professional judgement when marking, recognising that children often write more words than the brief, crisp answers given in the mark scheme.
Capital letters are not required unless specifically stated in the mark scheme.
Do not penalise spelling: as long as the meaning is clear, always award the mark.
Where a question asks for, say, 3 answers ticked and a pupil ticks 4, deduct one mark.

PiRA 5 Autumn

	Great Escapes	Mark	Level	Profile (AF)
1	70 minutes 2 mins 37 secs *accept* 2 mins 37 *or* 2.37 mins *Answers may be written or in figures, but units must be given.*	1 1	2a 2a	L (AF2) L (AF2)
2	1	1	2a	L (AF2)
3	Buried alive 4 Underwater 3 Handcuff Challenge 1 *All required for the mark.*	1	3c	A (AF4)
4	flicked	1	3a	A (AF5)
5	skyward	1	3a	A (AF5)
6	*Any two from:* immersed submerged surface pool (*do not accept* swimming, *accept* swimming pool)	1 1	4c 4c	A (AF5) A (AF5)
7				

		T	F	DNS
Houdini's stunts were very popular.	✓		
Houdini risked death in all his stunts		✓	
Houdini always performed in New York.		✓	

Marks: 1, 1, 1 — Levels 3a, 3b, 3c — M (AF3)

8	1926 – submerged 1904 – handcuff 1908 – straitjacket	1 1 1	3b 3b 3b	L (AF2) L (AF2) L (AF2)
9	*Any two from:* exhausted panicked unconscious	1 1	4c 4c	M (AF3) M (AF3)
	total	16		

	Lucky Escape			
10	prowling	1	3b	A (AF5)
11	1 4 Tiger is shot with a dart. 2 Waitress enters cafeteria. 3 Vet arrives. 6 5 Tiger falls asleep. *All in correct order for the mark.*	1	4b	L (AF2)

PiRA 5 mark schemes   49

12	*Any two from:* Staff were immediately evacuated *(accept* evacuated*)* Vet with tranquiliser gun *(accept* armed *or* gun *or* tranquiliser *or* special dart*)* Vet on site within 10 minutes *(accept* vet arrives quickly*)*	1 1	3a 3a	M (AF3) M (AF3)
13	she was heavy	1	2a	M (AF3)
14	*Any two from:* attacked chased mauled *or* injured *or* hurt *or* bit *(do not accept* knocked unconscious*)* eaten *or* killed *or* died	1 1	3c 3c	M (AF3) M (AF3)
15	sub-headings ✓ quotation ✓	1 1	3b 3b	A (AF4) A (AF4)
	total	9		

Crossing the Canyon

16		T	F	DNS	
	Juan has escaped from somewhere.	✓			
	Juan is running away from the lights.	✓			1	4c	M (AF3)
	Juan is running through a town.			✓	1	4c	M (AF3)
	Juan can hear dogs chasing him.		✓		
	2 marks for three or four correct; 1 mark for one or two correct				
17	felt like swallowing swords *(accept* swallowing swords*)*	1	3b	A (AF5)
18	*Any two from:* ran a long way ran for a long time ran very fast *Both required for the mark.*	1	3c	A (AF5)
19	*Any two from:* fear uncertainty hopes *Both required for the mark.*	1	4c	A (AF5)
20	brings us to an abrupt stop, like Juan	1	5c	A (AF4)
21	wide *or* big *or* huge	1	3a	M (AF3)
22	*Any one from:* he is despairing. he is worn out.	1	4a	M (AF3)
23	*Any one from:* leap *or* jump wait *(accept* get caught*)* give up, stay *or* go back	1	3c	L (AF2)
24(a)	2	1	3b	A (AF5)
24(b)	*Any one from:* impossible *or* not possible a dream pointless unlikely *or* slim *or* improbable *(accept* hard*)*	1	4b	M (AF3)
25	top left	1	3b	M (AF3)
26(a)	adventure	1	3b	A (AF7)
26(b)	excitement danger	1 1	4c 4c	A (AF7) A (AF7)
	total	15		
	Overall	40		

PiRA 5 Autumn: analysis

Pages and text type	Questions	Max mark	National average mark
2–3, non-fiction	1–9	16	9.2
4–5, report	10–15	9	4.0
6–8, story	16–26	15	6.6
PiRA Profile			
Literal comprehension		8	5.0
Reading for meaning		16	7.1
Appreciation of reading		16	7.6
	Total	40	19.9

PiRA 5 Spring

	A Small Dragon	Mark	Level	Profile (AF)
1	slips	1	3c	M (AF3)
2	brown *and* red Both required for the mark.	1	3b	M (AF3)
3	Any two from: needlepoint *(accept* needle*)* nails *or* rakes spiky *(note: three have been asked for allowing for a redundancy)*	1 1	4c 4c	M (AF3) M (AF3)
4	It makes the reader pause.	1	3b	A (AF5)
5	play *or* make friends	1	3a	M (AF3)
6	shouting	1	2a	A (AF4)
7	Any one from: bonfire soft earth smoke on the breeze *Accept* morning sun.	1	3b	M (AF3)
8	Any two from: needlepoint nails colourless crystal sniffs at wisps of smoke shell split *Accept* mouth, MUM *or* open onto	1 1	4c 4c	A (AF5) A (AF5)
9	disgusted	1	4a	A (AF6)
10	1 Dragon hatches from the egg. 4 Dragon wants to play. 2 Dragon changes colour. 3 Dragon tries out its claws. *All required for the mark.*	1	3a	M (AF3)
	total	12		

	The Yellow Dragon				Mark	Level	Profile (AF)
		T	F	DNS			
11	The Jade Emperor rules the world.	✓			1 1	3a 3a	L (AF2) L (AF2)
	The Yellow Dragon lives in the sky.		✓				
	People are suffering.	✓					
	The Emperor eats people's cakes.			✓			
	People are praying to the Jade Emperor.	✓					
	The Jade Emperor lives on the moon.		✓				
	1 mark for three or four correct, 2 marks for five or six correct.						
12	Paragraph 1 happy *and* lively Paragraph 2 sad *and* concerned Both required for each mark.	1 1	4c 4c	M (AF3) M (AF3)
13	Any one from: hungry starving sad thirsty *Accept 'ill'.*	1	3c	M (AF3)
14	to emphasise how far the dragon must fly	1	3b	A (AF5)
15(a)	magnificent palace *or* (plumply) cushioned couch	1	4b	M (AF3)
15(b)	Any one from: stared fiercely bellowed how dare you interrupt	1	4b	M (AF3)

PiRA 5 mark schemes

16	Any one from: heartless unstoppable	1	4c	A (AF5)
17	wings in tatters head hanging low Accept chained and bound.	1 1	3a 3a	L (AF2) L (AF2)
18	selfish cruel Both required for the mark.	1	4b	A (AF6)
19	mountain (accept rocks) river	1 1	3a 3a	L (AF2) L (AF2)
20	tells of a battle between good and evil gives explanations of nature	1 1	4b 4b	A (AF7) A (AF7)
21	to show that the story also links to today's beliefs	1	3b	A (AF4)
	total	17		
	Explorer's Journal			
22	eyes — leathery tongue — beady tail — snake-like All required for the mark.	1	2a	L (AF2)
23	getting information	1	4b	M (AF3)
24	over 2 metres (unit required) (accept 2 metres/meters) 11 mph (unit required) deer claws and teeth (accept speed or striking quickly for either) excellent (do not accept good) in/during the afternoon 1 mark for each three correct.	1 1	3a 3a	L (AF2) L (AF2)
25	compares know	1 1	4a 4a	A (AF5) A (AF5)
26	Any two from: a rare experience (a creature from) the time of the dinosaurs only 1100 left	1 1	3b 3b	A (AF6) A (AF6)
27	report – dangerous poem – colourful myth – honourable	1 1 1	5c 5c 5c	A (AF6) A (AF6) A (AF6)
	total	11		
	Overall	40		

PiRA 5 Spring: analysis

Pages and text type	Questions	Max mark	National average mark
2–3, poem	1–10	12	7.1
4–6, story	11–21	17	7.3
7–8, recount	22–27	11	4.5
PiRA Profile			
Literal comprehension		9	4.2
Reading for meaning		13	6.4
Appreciation of reading		18	8.3
	Total	40	18.9

PiRA 5 Summer

	The birthday	Mark	Level	Profile (AF)
1	*Any two from:* hats beards moustaches eye patches *Both required for the mark.*	1	2a	L (AF2)
2	films	1	3a	M (AF3)
3	False True Doesn't say. *All three required for the mark.*	1	3b	M (AF3)
4	emphasise annoyed *Both required for the mark.*	1	4b	A (AF4)
5	[in a bored way]	1	3b	M (AF3)
6	pause after each word	1	4c	A (AF5)
7	waving his sword	1	3b	M (AF3)
8	listening	1	4b	M (AF3)
9	light-hearted	1	4b	A (AF6)
10	full of energy bossy selfish *All three required for the mark.*	1	4b	M (AF3)
	total	10		
	The Pirate Crew			
11	Cecco — has lots of tattoos Bill Jukes — worked in a school Gentleman Starkey — pleasant man Smee — strange hands Noodler — wears gold coins. *2 marks for three, four or five correct;* *1 mark for one or two correct.*	1 1	3a 3a	L (AF2) L (AF2)
12	shied at — thug dainty — famous ruffian — is scared of long known — fussy *2 marks for three or four correct;* *1 mark for one or two correct*	1 1	4a 4a	A (AF5) A (AF5)
13(a)	hand *and* iron *Both required for the mark.*	1	3c	L (AF2)
13(b)	his own (*accept* his *or* own) blood	1 1	3b 3b	L (AF2) L (AF2)
14	*Any two from:* hook with which he encouraged them threatening expression to his handsome face never more terrifying than when he was most polite	1 1	4b 4b	A (AF5) A (AF5)
15	dogs *and* horses (*both required for the mark*)	1	3b	L (AF2)
16	They are really very sad. They are the colour of a flower. *Both required for the mark.*	1	3b	M (AF3)

PiRA 5 mark schemes

17	blue iris red pupil *Both required for the mark.*					1	3c	L (AF2)
18			T	F	NG	1 1	4c 4c	M (AF3) M (AF3)
	He is ugly.			✓				
	He is obeyed by his crew.		✓					
	He uses his hook for eating.				✓			
	When he is polite, he is particularly scary.		✓					
	He swore all the time.				✓			
	2 marks for four or five correct; *1 mark for two or three correct.*							
19	About the crew 1 and 2 About Hook 4 and 5 About both 3 only					1 1 1	5c 5c 5c	A (AF4) A (AF4) A (AF4)
20	the Italian (*or* Cecco) *and* Hook (*both required for the mark*)					1	3b	L (AF2)
					total	18		

PIRATE PARTIES

21	place					1	4c	M (AF3)
22			younger		older	1	3c	L (AF2)
	high plank				✓			
	paddling pool			✓				
	bouncy cushion				✓			
	toy crocodile			✓				
	All four required for the mark.							
23	lay out the food					1	4c	M (AF3)
24			T	F	DNS	1 1	4c 4c	M (AF3) M (AF3)
	Pirate parties are expensive.				✓			
	Parents have to help with the party.			✓				
	The games are just for small children.			✓				
	Pin the Patch on the Pirate is an enjoyable game.		✓					
	You eat the party food with your hands.		✓					
	2 marks for four or five correct; *1 mark for two or three correct.*							
25	rhyme engage					1 1	4a 4a	A (AF4) A (AF4)
26	sub-headings ——— tells you briefly … alliteration ⟋ eye-catching drawings ⤫ makes it easy to contact… link to email ⟍ makes the message more…. *2 marks for three or four correct.* *1 mark for one or two correct.*					1 1	4a 4a	A (AF4) A (AF4)
27	informal language second person					1 1	4a 4a	A (AF7)
28			Fun	Scary	Both	1	4b	A (AF6)
	The Birthday			✓				
	The Pirate Crew				✓			
	Pirate Parties					✓		
	1 mark for two or three correct.							
					total	12		
					Overall	40		

PiRA 5 mark schemes   55

PiRA 5 Summer: analysis

Pages and text type	Questions	Max mark	National average mark
2–3, playscript	1–10	10	5.5
4–5, story	11–20	18	9.7
6–8, advert	21–28	12	6.2
PiRA Profile			
Literal comprehension		10	6.5
Reading for meaning		13	7.7
Appreciation of reading		17	7.3
	Total	40	21.5

PiRA Answers & Mark Schemes: PiRA 6

Please use professional judgement when marking, recognising that children often write more words than the brief, crisp answers given in the mark scheme.
Capital letters are not required unless specifically stated in the mark scheme.
Do not penalise spelling: as long as the meaning is clear, always award the mark.
Where a question asks for, say, 3 answers ticked and a pupil ticks 4, deduct one mark.

PiRA 6 Autumn

	Letter about Kayaking				Mark	Level	Profile (AF)
1	They rushed excitedly.				1	3a	A (AF5)
2		T	F	DNS			
	There is a swimming pool near their home.	✓			1	4c	M (AF3)
	The children are on holiday with their grandparents.		✓		1	4c	M (AF3)
3	Any two from: float have mini-races *or* race paddle snake round bends *Do not accept* enjoy the countryside.				1 1	3c 3c	L (AF2) L (AF2)
4	Any two from: puffing panting red-faced				1 1	3b 3b	M (AF3) M (AF3)
5	cows, sheep, geese These three **only** and no others for the mark.				1	3b	L (AF2)
				total	8		
	Keeping Joe Busy						
6	Joe is — 2, 5 ; Danny is — 6, 11, 12				1	3c	M (AF3)
7	end of the garden (*accept* back of garden; *do not accept* garden)				1	3c	L (AF2)
8	crouched (*do not accept* concentrating)				1	3a	M (AF3)
9	silvery *or* silver thin (*accept* 'length of my thumb') *Both required for the mark*				1	3b	A (AF5)
10	to show speed to show movement				1 1	4a 4a	A (AF5) A (AF5)
11	absorbed hypnotised				1 1	4a 4a	A (AF5) A (AF5)
12	imagine them clearly understand why the boys are so fascinated				1 1	4b 4b	A (AF6) A (AF6)
13	to signal a turning point in the story to change the atmosphere of the story				1 1	5c 5c	A (AF4) A (AF4)
14	cold If cold *and* nervous both circled, ignore nervous and award mark				1	3a	M (AF3)

PiRA 6 mark schemes 57

15	worried				1	3a	A (AF4)
16	fish *Do not accept* water ripples.				1	4b	M (AF3)
17	Danny on hearing Mum's instruction — babyish boy / frightened of him / talkative nuisance Danny as he is climbing out of the stream — panicking concern Danny finding Joe on mother's lap — *either* bored by him / predictable boy				1 1 1	4a 4a 4a	M (AF3) M (AF3) M (AF3)
18	3 Joe sees the fish. 5 Danny searches for Joe. 4 Danny scares the fish. 1 It rains heavily. *All in the correct order for the mark.*				1	4b	L (AF2)
19		T	F	DNS			
	It gives a happy ending.	✓			1	4a	A (AF6)
	It shows that Mum knew I had been worried.		✓		1	4a	A (AF6)
	It shows that Mum had been very busy.			✓	1	4a	A (AF6)
				total	22		

Otter Info

20	Many otters died in the 1960s. ✓ Otters die from eating poisoned fish. ✓ Otters are sometimes killed by traffic. ✓ Sometimes there is not enough food for otters. ✓ *2 marks for three or four correct answers;* *1 mark for one or two correct answers.*	1 1	4c 4c	L (AF2) L (AF2)
21	Fish is the main source of food for otters. ✓ Otters sometimes build homes in riverbanks. ✓ Female otters do not travel as far as male otters. ✓ Otters sometimes use the homes of other creatures ✓ *2 marks for three or four correct;* *1 mark for one or two correct.*	1 1	4b 4b	L (AF2) L (AF2)
22	nocturnal	1	3a	M (AF3)
23	holt	1	3c	L (AF2)
24	banned	1	3a	M (AF3)
25	to make us aware of how threatened otters are. to help us to understand how humans affect nature. *Both required for the mark.*	1	4c	A (AF4)
26	to inform the reader about otters.	1	3a	A (AF6)

27	Description	Kayaking Letter	Keeping Joe Busy	Otter Info			
	Fish are important.		✓	✓	1	4b	A (AF7)
	It is mainly about people.	✓	✓				
	It is mainly about animals.			✓			
	1 mark for 4 or 5 boxes ticked, with no incorrect ones ticked.						
				total	10		
				Overall	40		

PiRA 6 Autumn: analysis

Pages and text type	Questions	Max mark	National average mark
2, letter	1–5	8	5.1
3–5, story	6–19	22	12.1
6–8, non-fiction	20–27	10	6.6
PiRA Profile			
Literal comprehension		10	7.0
Reading for meaning		13	7.4
Appreciation of reading		17	9.3
	Total	40	23.5

PiRA 6 Spring

	Transforming the School Playground	Mark	Level	Profile (AF)
1	bored	1	3a	M (AF3)
2	Any two from: flowers *or* wildlife ideas for poems *or* writing study of insects *or* plants *or* for science something with maths outdoor classroom *Do not accept 'break times'.*	1 1	3b 3b	L (AF2) L (AF2)
3	to make her audience think	1	5c	A (AF5)
4	giving examples	1	4c	A (AF6)
5	Any one from: less space for football less space for big games not everyone likes chatting not everyone likes sitting *Do not accept 'Don't want a nature garden', or unqualified references to football or games or chatting or sitting.*	1	3a	M (AF3)
6(a)	On the other hand	1	4c	A (AF6)
6(b)	And another thing	1	4c	A (AF6)
7	1 — to introduce the idea and excite the audience 2 — to involve all pupils with the nature garden 3 — to argue for more space for running games — to recognise other children may want to use the space differently *1 mark for two or three correct.*	1	4a	A (AF6)
8	to explain that it will be good for everyone	1	4c	A (AF6)
	total	10		
	Merlin and the Snake's Egg			
9	Merlin Glain *Both required for the mark.*	1	3c	L (AF2)
10	cress herbs twig *All required for the mark.*	1	3c	L (AF2)
11	Any two from: takes place at night *or* in dark *or* night thick as soot fire is low wind is still or at rest dog moans bad dreams	1 1	4c 4c	A (AF6) A (AF6)
12	dangerous	1	3b	A (AF5)
13	Any two from: salmon *(accept* fish*)* spider owl *(accept* bird*)* *Both required for the mark.*	1	3b	L (AF2)
14	cut	1	3a	M (AF3)
15	to increase your interest and anticipation	1	4b	A (AF5)
16	loud – His voice one of night's alarms quiet – Silent and soft he flies *Precise quotations required, apart from the capital letters and punctuation.*	1 1	4a 4a	M (AF3) M (AF3)

17	alliteration: steadfastly searches *or* last light leans simile: like a little moon	1 1	5b 5b	A (AF5) A (AF5)
18	4 goes to the wood 9 2 rests 1 learns and read 3 6 swims 7 crawls 5 8 flies *1 mark for five or six correct.*	1	4c	M (AF3)
	total	13		
	A lesson in life			
19	a machine to create life	1	4c	M (AF3)
20		The narrator …	T	F	DNS
---	---	---	---
is a girl			✓
is human		✓	
likes to play laserball	✓		
can hover	✓		

2 marks for three or four correct;
1 mark for one or two correct. | 1
1 | 4a
4a | L (AF2)
L (AF2) |
21	dumb primitive	1 1	3b	M (AF3)
22	to express superiority	1	4b	A (AF6)
23	*Any three from:* colour of the sky laser ball game turning water into a human speed pods humans are undeveloped creatures now do not walk on the ground now do not talk to communicate now do not eat food *Accept it is 4092 (or the year it is now)*	1 1 1	4b 4b 4b	M (AF3) M (AF3) M (AF3)
24	laser mirror Change-o-Matic test tube (of water) *Do not accept 'beam' but ignore it if it is a fifth label.* *1 mark for three or four correct labels.*	1	4c	L (AF2)
25	The narrator is thinking.	1	4c	A (AF4)
26	exploded – suddenly turned riot – many colours	1 1	4b	A (AF5)
27	engaged pleased worried *All required for the mark.*	1	4b	M (AF3)
28	Transforming the School Playground — magical / real Merlin and the Snake's Egg — adventure A Lesson in Life — historical / scientific *Two lines from any title negate that mark, but do not penalise other lines.*	1 1 1	4b 4b 4b	A (AF7) A (AF7) A (AF7)
	total	17		
	Overall	40		

PiRA 6 Spring: analysis

Pages and text type	Questions	Max mark	National average mark
2–3, persuasive	1–8	10	5.8
4–5, poem	9–18	13	9.0
6–8, story	19–28	17	8.2
PiRA Profile			
Literal comprehension		8	5.5
Reading for meaning		13	7.0
Appreciation of reading		19	10.4
	Total	40	23.0

PiRA 6 Summer

	The Secret Caves of Cozumel	Mark	Level	Profile (AF)
1	Mexico 7 *or* seven *Both required for the mark.*	1	3c	L (AF2)
2	Mayan people *or* Mayans	1	3a	L (AF2)
3	green *and* glowing *Both required for the mark. Ignore any other extra descriptions.*	1	3c	L (AF2)
4	roots *(do not accept* trees*)*	1	3a	L (AF2)
5	enchanting — size mysterious — beauty piercing — brightness eerie — massive illuminating — huge (**mysterious**, **size**, **beauty**, **brightness** shown in bold) 3 marks for all six correct; 2 marks for four or five correct; 1 mark for two or three correct.	1 1 1	3c 4c 5c	A (AF6) A (AF6) A (AF6)
6	*Any two from:* They are difficult to get into. They are deep underground. Very few people visit them.	1 1	4c 4c	M (AF3) M (AF3)
7	*Any three from:* hole light *or* beam of light; *accept* hazy light roots stalactites pool *or* water *or* green pool stairs *or* steps ledge *or* slippery ledge chamber canopy *or* ooze rock *Any three correct labels written on, linked to or alongside the correct position.*	1	3b	L (AF2)
8	*Any two from:* impressive fascinating unique imposing	1 1	4c 4c	A (AF5) A (AF5)
9	To make readers wonder what the secret is. To reinforce how special the secret is. *Both required for the mark.*	1	5c	A (AF4)
	total	13		
	Can you keep a secret?			
10	Jo — teacher Mrs Alonso — mother Carmella — daughter Kevin — postman Karen — neighbour *All five required for the mark.*	1	3b	L (AF2)
11	*Any one from:* Carmella *or* anyone does not hear her *or* no one can hear Carmella *or* anyone is not listening. Carmella *or* anyone is not there *or* behind her *or* no one is there *(Do not accept* Camella is not looking.*)*	1	4b	M (AF3)

12	pause *or* hesitate *Accept* stop *or* to look like she is thinking *or* take a breath.	1	4b	A (AF5)
13	hurriedly noisily dramatically *All three required for the mark.*	1	4a	A (AF6)
14	doesn't expect expects expects *2 marks for three correct; 1 mark for two correct.*	1 1	5c 5c	A (AF5) A (AF5)
15	2 let down 1 surprise 4 triumph 3 despair *2 marks for four correct; 1 mark for any two correct.*	1 1	5b 5b	M (AF3) M (AF3)
16	audition Make Me a Star *(capitals not essential)* will *or* would *or* must *or* should *(do not accept* could*)* *2 marks for three correct; 1 mark for two correct.*	1 1	3b 4a	L (AF2) M (AF3)
	total	10		
	The man behind James Bond			
17	*Any one from:* spying secrecy	1	3a	M (AF3)
18	1908 *(not just 'May')* Peter Sandhurst; *accept* Military Academy 23 1953 In the second world war or WW2 *(do not accept* 1939*).* *3 marks for all six correct;* *2 marks for three, four or five correct;* *1 mark for one or two correct*	1 1 1	3c 4b 4a	L (AF2) L (AF2) L (AF2)
19	doesn't say true true	1 1 1	4c 4b 4a	M (AF3) M (AF3) M (AF3)
20	manner *or* style gift *or* liking rules *or* work	1 1 1	4b 4b 4b	M (AF3) M (AF3) M (AF3)
21	'Asked' is a polite way to say 'told'.	1	5c	A (AF4)
22	2 4 5 6 circled *2 marks for the correct four circled only.* *1 mark for any two or three correctly circled (even if one or two others are incorrectly circled).*	1 1	5b 5b	A (AF4) A (AF4)
23	*Any two from:* the secret service *or* Naval intelligence *or* spy skills secret codes exchanging important prisoners gold-smuggling deep-sea exploration criminal networks dangerous missions *(Do not accept* travelling *or* war experience.*)*	1	4b	M (AF3)
24	prepare	1	4c	A (AF5)
25	travel guide playscript biography *(do not accept* autobiography*)* *2 marks for all three correct; 1 mark for two correct.*	1 1	4b 4b	A (AF7) A (AF7)
	total	17		
	Overall	**40**		

PiRA 6 Summer: analysis

Pages and text type	Questions	Max mark	National average mark
2–3, brochure	1–9	13	8.4
4–5, playscript	10–16	10	5.0
6–8, non-fiction	17–25	17	9.0
PiRA Profile			
Literal comprehension		10	7.2
Reading for meaning		14	7.3
Appreciation of reading		16	7.9
	Total	40	22.5

PiRA Standardised Score conversion tables

Age in years and months

Raw Score	6:5	6:6	6:7	6:8	6:9	6:10	6:11	7:0	7:1	7:2	7:3	7:4	7:5	7:6	7:7	7:8	Raw Score
1	77	76	75	74	73	72	71	70									1
2	80	79	78	78	77	76	76	75	75	74	73	72	71	70	70		2
3	82	82	81	80	80	79	78	78	77	77	76	76	76	75	74	73	3
4	84	83	83	82	82	81	81	80	79	79	78	78	77	77	77	76	4
5	85	85	85	84	83	83	82	82	81	81	80	80	79	79	78	78	5
6	87	86	86	85	85	84	84	83	83	82	82	81	81	81	80	80	6
7	88	87	87	86	86	85	85	85	84	84	83	83	82	82	82	81	7
8	89	88	88	87	87	87	86	86	85	85	85	84	84	83	83	82	8
9	90	90	89	89	88	88	87	87	86	86	86	85	85	85	84	84	9
10	91	91	90	90	89	89	88	88	87	87	87	86	86	85	85	85	10
11	93	92	92	91	90	90	89	89	88	88	87	87	87	86	86	86	11
12	94	93	93	92	92	91	91	90	90	89	89	88	88	87	87	87	12
13	94	94	94	93	93	92	92	91	91	90	90	89	89	88	88	87	13
14	95	95	95	94	94	93	93	92	92	91	91	90	90	89	89	88	14
15	96	96	95	95	95	94	94	93	93	93	92	92	91	91	90	90	15
16	97	97	96	96	96	95	95	94	94	93	93	93	92	92	91	91	16
17	98	97	97	97	96	96	96	95	95	94	94	94	93	93	92	92	17
18	99	98	98	97	97	97	96	96	96	95	95	95	94	94	93	93	18
19	100	99	99	98	98	98	97	97	97	96	96	95	95	95	94	94	19
20	101	100	100	99	99	99	98	98	97	97	97	96	96	96	95	95	20
21	102	101	101	101	100	100	99	99	98	98	98	97	97	96	96	96	21
22	103	103	102	102	101	101	100	100	99	99	98	98	98	97	97	97	22
23	104	104	103	103	102	102	102	101	101	100	100	99	99	98	98	97	23
24	106	105	105	104	104	103	103	102	102	101	101	100	100	99	99	98	24
25	107	107	106	106	105	105	104	104	103	103	102	102	101	101	100	100	25
26	108	108	107	107	107	106	106	105	105	104	104	103	103	102	102	101	26
27	109	109	109	108	108	108	107	107	106	106	105	105	104	104	103	102	27
28	111	111	110	110	109	109	109	108	108	107	107	106	106	106	105	104	28
29	113	113	112	112	111	111	110	110	109	109	108	108	107	107	107	106	29
30	115	114	114	114	113	113	112	112	111	111	110	110	109	109	108	108	30
31	116	116	115	115	115	115	114	114	114	113	113	112	112	111	110	110	31
32	118	118	118	117	117	117	116	116	115	115	115	114	114	113	113	112	32
33	120	120	120	120	119	119	119	118	118	117	117	117	116	115	115	115	33
34	122	122	122	122	122	121	121	121	121	120	120	119	119	119	118	118	34
35	125	124	124	124	124	124	123	123	123	123	123	122	122	122	121	121	35
36	127	127	127	127	127	127	126	126	126	126	126	125	125	125	124	124	36
37	130	130	130	130	130	130	130	130	130	130	130	129	129	129	129	129	37
38																	38
39				SCORE 130+ IN THIS AREA													39
40																	40
	6:5	6:6	6:7	6:8	6:9	6:10	6:11	7:0	7:1	7:2	7:3	7:4	7:5	7:6	7:7	7:8	

PiRA 3 Autumn standardised scores

PiRA 3 Autumn

Age in years and months

Raw Score	7:9	7:10	7:11	8:0	8:1	8:2	8:3	8:4	8:5	8:6	8:7	8:8	8:9	8:10	8:11	9:0	Raw Score
1																	1
2									SCORE 70- IN THIS AREA								2
3	73	72	71	71	70	70	69										3
4	76	76	75	75	74	73	73	72	72	71	71	70	70	69			4
5	78	77	77	76	76	76	76	75	75	74	74	73	73	72	72	71	5
6	79	79	78	78	78	77	77	77	76	76	76	76	75	75	74	74	6
7	81	80	80	79	79	79	78	78	78	77	77	77	77	76	76	76	7
8	82	82	81	81	81	80	80	79	79	79	78	78	78	78	77	77	8
9	83	83	82	82	82	81	81	81	80	80	80	79	79	79	78	78	9
10	84	84	84	83	83	82	82	82	81	81	81	81	80	80	80	79	10
11	85	85	85	84	84	84	83	83	83	82	82	82	81	81	81	80	11
12	86	86	86	85	85	85	84	84	84	83	83	83	82	82	82	81	12
13	87	87	86	86	86	85	85	85	85	84	84	84	83	83	83	82	13
14	88	88	87	87	87	86	86	86	85	85	85	84	84	84	83	83	14
15	89	89	88	88	87	87	87	86	86	86	85	85	85	85	84	84	15
16	90	90	89	89	88	88	87	87	87	86	86	86	86	85	85	85	16
17	91	91	90	90	89	89	88	88	88	87	87	87	86	86	86	86	17
18	92	92	91	91	90	90	89	89	89	88	88	87	87	87	86	86	18
19	93	93	92	92	92	91	91	90	90	89	89	88	88	88	87	87	19
20	94	94	93	93	93	92	92	91	91	90	90	89	89	88	88	88	20
21	95	95	94	94	94	93	93	92	92	91	91	90	90	89	89	89	21
22	96	96	95	95	94	94	94	93	93	92	92	91	91	90	90	90	22
23	97	97	96	96	95	95	95	94	94	93	93	92	92	91	91	91	23
24	98	98	97	97	96	96	96	95	95	94	94	93	93	93	92	92	24
25	99	99	98	98	97	97	97	96	96	95	95	94	94	93	93	93	25
26	101	100	99	99	98	98	97	97	97	96	96	95	95	94	94	94	26
27	102	101	101	100	100	99	99	98	98	97	97	96	96	95	95	95	27
28	104	103	102	102	101	101	100	99	99	98	98	97	97	96	96	96	28
29	106	105	104	103	103	102	102	101	100	100	99	99	98	98	97	97	29
30	107	107	106	106	105	104	103	103	102	101	101	100	99	99	98	98	30
31	109	109	108	107	107	106	106	105	104	103	103	102	101	101	100	99	31
32	112	111	110	110	109	108	108	107	106	106	105	104	103	102	102	101	32
33	114	114	113	113	112	111	110	109	109	108	107	107	106	105	104	103	33
34	117	116	116	115	115	114	114	113	112	111	110	109	108	108	107	106	34
35	121	120	120	119	119	118	117	116	116	115	114	113	113	111	110	109	35
36	124	124	123	123	123	122	122	121	121	120	119	118	117	116	115	114	36
37	129	129	128	128	128	128	127	127	126	126	125	125	124	124	123	122	37
38															130	129	38
39																	39
40																	40
	7:9	7:10	7:11	8:0	8:1	8:2	8:3	8:4	8:5	8:6	8:7	8:8	8:9	8:10	8:11	9:0	

PiRA 3 Autumn standardised scores

PiRA 3 Spring

PiRA 3 Spring standardised scores

Age in years and months

Raw Score	7:0	7:1	7:2	7:3	7:4	7:5	7:6	7:7	7:8	7:9	7:10	7:11	8:0	Raw Score
1	74	74	73	72	72	71	71	70	69					1
2	76	76	75	75	74	73	73	72	72	71	71	70	70	2
3	78	78	77	77	76	76	75	74	74	73	73	72	72	3
4	80	79	79	78	78	77	77	76	76	75	75	74	74	4
5	82	81	81	80	80	79	78	78	77	77	76	76	76	5
6	83	83	82	82	81	81	80	80	79	79	78	78	77	6
7	85	84	84	83	83	82	82	81	81	80	80	79	79	7
8	86	86	85	85	84	84	83	83	82	82	81	81	80	8
9	88	87	87	86	86	85	85	84	84	83	83	82	82	9
10	89	88	88	88	87	87	86	86	85	85	84	84	83	10
11	90	90	89	89	88	88	87	87	86	86	85	85	84	11
12	91	91	90	90	90	89	89	88	88	87	87	86	86	12
13	92	92	91	91	91	90	90	89	89	89	88	88	87	13
14	93	93	92	92	91	91	91	90	90	90	89	89	88	14
15	95	94	94	93	93	92	92	91	91	91	90	90	90	15
16	96	96	95	95	94	94	93	92	92	92	91	91	91	16
17	98	97	97	96	96	95	95	94	93	93	92	92	91	17
18	99	99	98	98	97	97	96	95	95	94	94	93	93	18
19	100	100	99	99	99	98	98	97	96	96	95	95	94	19
20	102	101	101	100	100	99	99	98	98	97	97	96	96	20
21	103	103	102	102	101	101	100	100	99	99	98	98	97	21
22	105	105	104	103	103	102	101	101	100	100	99	99	99	22
23	107	106	106	105	104	104	103	102	102	101	101	100	100	23
24	109	108	107	107	106	106	105	104	104	103	102	102	101	24
25	110	110	109	109	108	107	107	106	106	105	104	104	103	25
26	112	112	111	110	110	109	109	108	107	107	106	105	105	26
27	114	113	113	112	112	111	110	110	109	109	108	107	107	27
28	116	116	115	114	114	113	112	112	111	111	110	109	109	28
29	118	118	117	116	116	115	115	114	113	112	112	111	111	29
30	120	120	119	119	118	117	117	116	115	115	114	113	113	30
31	123	122	122	121	120	120	119	118	118	117	116	116	115	31
32	126	125	124	124	123	122	122	121	120	119	119	118	117	32
33	130	129	128	127	126	125	124	124	123	122	121	121	120	33
34					130	129	128	127	126	125	124	124	123	34
35										130	129	128	127	126	35
36														36
37														37
38				SCORE 130+ IN THIS AREA										38
39														39
40														40
	7:0	7:1	7:2	7:3	7:4	7:5	7:6	7:7	7:8	7:9	7:10	7:11	8:0	

PiRA 3 Spring

Age in years and months

Raw Score	8:1	8:2	8:3	8:4	8:5	8:6	8:7	8:8	8:9	8:10	8:11	9:0	9:1	Raw Score
1														1
2						SCORE 70- IN THIS AREA								2
3	71	71	70	70										3
4	73	73	72	72	71	71	70	70						4
5	75	75	74	73	73	72	72	71	71	71	70	70		5
6	77	76	76	75	75	74	74	73	73	72	72	71	71	6
7	78	78	77	77	76	76	76	75	75	74	74	73	73	7
8	80	79	79	78	78	77	77	77	76	76	75	75	74	8
9	81	81	80	80	79	79	78	78	78	77	77	76	76	9
10	83	82	82	81	81	80	80	79	79	79	78	78	77	10
11	84	84	83	83	82	82	81	81	80	80	80	79	79	11
12	85	85	84	84	83	83	83	82	82	81	81	81	80	12
13	87	86	86	85	85	84	84	83	83	83	82	82	81	13
14	88	88	87	87	86	86	85	85	84	84	83	83	83	14
15	89	89	88	88	87	87	87	86	86	85	85	84	84	15
16	90	90	89	89	89	88	88	87	87	86	86	85	85	16
17	91	91	90	90	90	89	89	89	88	88	87	87	86	17
18	92	92	91	91	91	90	90	90	89	89	88	88	88	18
19	94	93	92	92	92	91	91	91	90	90	90	89	89	19
20	95	95	94	93	93	92	92	91	91	91	90	90	90	20
21	97	96	95	95	94	94	93	92	92	92	91	91	91	21
22	98	98	97	96	96	95	95	94	94	93	92	92	92	22
23	99	99	98	98	97	97	96	96	95	95	94	93	93	23
24	101	100	100	99	99	98	98	97	97	96	95	95	94	24
25	102	102	101	101	100	100	99	99	98	98	97	96	96	25
26	104	103	103	102	101	101	100	100	99	99	98	98	97	26
27	106	105	105	104	103	103	102	101	101	100	100	99	99	27
28	108	107	107	106	105	105	104	103	102	102	101	101	100	28
29	110	109	109	108	107	107	106	105	105	104	103	102	102	29
30	112	111	111	110	109	109	108	107	107	106	105	104	104	30
31	114	113	113	112	111	111	110	109	109	108	107	107	106	31
32	117	116	115	114	114	113	112	112	111	110	109	109	108	32
33	119	118	118	117	116	116	115	114	113	112	112	111	110	33
34	122	121	120	120	119	118	117	117	116	115	114	113	112	34
35	125	124	124	123	122	121	120	119	118	118	117	116	115	35
36	130	129	128	127	126	124	124	123	122	121	120	119	118	36
37					130	129	128	127	126	124	124	123	122	37
38										130	128	127	126	38
39														39
40														40
	8:1	8:2	8:3	8:4	8:5	8:6	8:7	8:8	8:9	8:10	8:11	9:0	9:1	

PiRA 3 Spring standardised scores

PiRA 3 Summer

PiRA 3 Summer standardised scores

Age in years and months

Raw Score	7:3	7:4	7:5	7:6	7:7	7:8	7:9	7:10	7:11	8:0	8:1	8:2	8:3	Raw Score
1														1
2														2
3	70	70	70			SCORE 70- IN THIS AREA								3
4	71	71	71	71	71	71	70	70	70	70	70	70		4
5	73	73	72	72	72	72	72	72	72	72	72	71	71	5
6	74	74	74	74	74	74	74	74	74	74	73	73	73	6
7	75	75	75	75	75	75	75	75	75	75	75	75	75	7
8	77	77	77	77	77	77	77	77	77	77	77	77	77	8
9	80	79	79	79	79	79	79	79	78	78	78	78	78	9
10	82	81	81	81	81	81	80	80	80	80	80	80	80	10
11	84	83	83	83	82	82	82	82	82	81	81	81	81	11
12	85	85	85	84	84	84	84	83	83	83	83	82	82	12
13	87	87	86	86	86	85	85	85	85	84	84	84	84	13
14	89	88	88	88	87	87	87	86	86	86	86	85	85	14
15	90	90	89	89	89	88	88	88	88	87	87	87	86	15
16	92	91	91	90	90	90	89	89	89	89	88	88	88	16
17	93	93	92	92	92	91	91	90	90	90	89	89	89	17
18	94	94	93	93	93	93	92	92	92	91	91	91	90	18
19	96	95	95	94	94	94	93	93	93	93	92	92	92	19
20	97	97	97	96	96	95	95	94	94	94	93	93	93	20
21	99	99	98	98	97	97	96	96	95	95	94	94	94	21
22	101	100	100	99	99	99	98	98	97	97	96	96	95	22
23	103	102	102	101	101	100	100	99	99	98	98	98	97	23
24	104	104	104	103	103	102	102	101	101	100	100	99	99	24
25	106	106	105	105	105	104	104	103	103	102	102	101	101	25
26	108	108	107	107	106	106	105	105	105	104	104	103	103	26
27	110	110	109	109	109	108	108	107	107	106	105	105	105	27
28	113	112	112	111	110	110	110	109	109	108	108	107	107	28
29	115	115	114	114	113	113	113	112	111	111	110	110	109	29
30	117	117	116	116	116	116	115	115	114	114	113	113	112	30
31	119	118	118	118	118	117	117	117	117	116	116	116	115	31
32	121	121	121	120	120	119	119	119	119	118	118	118	117	32
33	124	124	124	123	123	123	122	122	122	121	121	120	120	33
34	128	127	127	127	127	126	126	126	125	125	125	124	124	34
35				130	130	130	130	130	130	129	129	129	129	35
36														36
37														37
38					SCORE 130+ IN THIS AREA									38
39														39
40														40
	7:3	7:4	7:5	7:6	7:7	7:8	7:9	7:10	7:11	8:0	8:1	8:2	8:3	

PiRA 3 Summer

Age in years and months

Raw Score	8:4	8:5	8:6	8:7	8:8	8:9	8:10	8:11	9:0	9:1	9:2	9:3	9:4	Raw Score
1														1
2														2
3														3
4														4
5	71	71	71	71	70	70	70	70	70	70	70	70	70	5
6	73	73	73	73	72	72	72	72	72	72	72	72	72	6
7	75	75	75	75	75	75	75	75	75	75	75	75	75	7
8	77	77	77	77	77	77	77	76	76	76	76	76	76	8
9	78	78	78	78	78	78	78	78	78	78	77	77	77	9
10	79	79	79	79	79	79	79	79	79	79	79	78	78	10
11	81	81	80	80	80	80	80	80	80	80	80	79	79	11
12	82	82	82	82	81	81	81	81	81	81	81	80	80	12
13	83	83	83	83	83	82	82	82	82	82	82	82	81	13
14	85	85	84	84	84	84	83	83	83	83	83	83	82	14
15	86	86	86	85	85	85	85	84	84	84	84	84	84	15
16	87	87	87	87	86	86	86	86	85	85	85	85	85	16
17	89	88	88	88	88	87	87	87	87	86	86	86	86	17
18	90	90	89	89	89	88	88	88	88	88	87	87	87	18
19	91	91	91	90	90	90	89	89	89	89	88	88	88	19
20	93	92	92	92	91	91	91	90	90	90	89	89	89	20
21	94	93	93	93	93	92	92	92	91	91	91	90	90	21
22	95	94	94	94	94	93	93	93	93	92	92	92	91	22
23	97	96	96	95	95	94	94	94	94	93	93	93	93	23
24	98	98	98	97	97	96	96	95	95	94	94	94	93	24
25	100	100	99	99	98	98	97	97	97	96	96	95	95	25
26	102	102	101	101	100	100	99	99	98	98	97	97	97	26
27	104	104	103	103	102	102	101	101	100	100	99	99	98	27
28	106	106	105	105	104	104	104	103	102	102	101	101	100	28
29	109	108	108	107	107	106	105	105	105	104	104	103	102	29
30	111	111	110	110	109	109	108	108	107	106	106	105	105	30
31	115	114	114	113	112	112	111	110	110	109	109	108	107	31
32	117	117	116	116	116	115	115	114	113	113	112	111	110	32
33	119	119	119	118	118	118	117	117	117	116	116	115	114	33
34	124	123	123	122	122	121	121	120	120	119	119	118	118	34
35	128	128	128	127	127	127	126	126	125	125	124	124	123	35
36													130	36
37														37
38														38
39														39
40														40
	8:4	8:5	8:6	8:7	8:8	8:9	8:10	8:11	9:0	9:1	9:2	9:3	9:4	

PiRA 3 Summer standardised scores

PiRA 4 Autumn

Age in years and months

Raw Score	7:4	7:5	7:6	7:7	7:8	7:9	7:10	7:11	8:0	8:1	8:2	8:3	8:4	8:5	8:6	8:7	8:8	Raw Score
1	72	70	70	70														1
2	76	75	74	73	72	72	72	71	71	71	70	70	70	70	70	70	70	2
3	82	81	80	79	78	78	77	77	76	76	76	75	75	74	74	74	73	3
4	86	85	84	83	82	82	81	80	80	79	79	78	78	78	77	77	77	4
5	89	88	88	87	86	85	84	83	83	82	82	81	81	80	80	79	79	5
6	92	91	90	89	89	88	87	86	86	85	84	84	83	83	82	82	81	6
7	94	93	92	91	91	90	89	89	88	88	87	86	85	85	84	84	83	7
8	96	95	94	94	93	92	91	91	90	89	89	88	88	87	87	86	85	8
9	98	97	96	96	95	94	93	93	92	91	91	90	90	89	88	88	88	9
10	100	99	98	98	97	96	95	95	94	93	92	92	91	91	90	90	89	10
11	102	101	100	99	99	98	97	96	96	95	94	94	93	92	92	91	91	11
12	103	102	102	101	100	100	99	98	97	97	96	95	95	94	93	93	92	12
13	104	103	103	102	102	101	100	100	99	98	98	97	96	96	95	94	94	13
14	105	105	104	104	103	103	102	101	101	100	99	99	98	97	97	96	95	14
15	106	106	105	105	104	104	103	103	102	102	101	100	99	99	98	97	97	15
16	107	107	106	106	106	105	104	104	103	103	102	102	101	100	100	99	98	16
17	108	108	107	107	107	106	106	105	105	104	103	103	102	102	101	101	100	17
18	110	109	109	108	108	107	107	106	106	105	105	104	104	103	103	102	101	18
19	111	110	110	109	109	108	108	107	107	106	106	105	105	104	104	103	103	19
20	112	112	111	111	110	110	109	108	108	107	107	106	106	106	105	104	104	20
21	113	113	112	112	111	111	110	110	109	109	108	108	107	107	106	106	105	21
22	115	114	114	113	113	112	112	111	111	110	109	109	108	108	107	107	106	22
23	116	115	115	114	114	114	113	112	112	111	111	110	110	109	108	108	107	23
24	117	117	116	116	115	115	114	114	113	113	112	112	111	110	110	109	109	24
25	119	118	118	117	117	116	116	115	115	114	114	113	112	112	111	111	110	25
26	120	119	119	119	118	118	117	117	116	115	115	114	114	113	113	112	112	26
27	121	121	121	120	120	119	119	118	118	117	116	116	115	115	114	114	113	27
28	123	123	122	122	121	121	120	120	119	119	118	118	117	116	116	115	115	28
29	124	124	124	123	123	122	122	121	121	120	120	119	119	118	118	117	116	29
30	127	126	126	125	124	124	124	123	123	122	122	121	121	120	119	119	118	30
31	130	129	128	128	127	127	126	125	125	124	124	123	123	122	121	121	120	31
32					130	129	129	128	128	127	126	125	125	124	123	123	122	32
33									130	129	129	128	127	126	125	125		33
34														130	129	128		34
35																		35
36																		36
37																		37
38							SCORE 130+ IN THIS AREA											38
39																		39
40																		40
	7:4	7:5	7:6	7:7	7:8	7:9	7:10	7:11	8:0	8:1	8:2	8:3	8:4	8:5	8:6	8:7	8:8	

PiRA 4 Autumn standardised scores

PiRA 4 Autumn

Age in years and months

Raw Score	8:9	8:10	8:11	9:0	9:1	9:2	9:3	9:4	9:5	9:6	9:7	9:8	9:9	9:10	9:11	10:0	Raw Score
1																	1
2						SCORE 70- IN THIS AREA											2
3	73	73	73	72	72	72	72	72	72	71	71	71	71	71	71	71	3
4	76	76	76	76	75	75	75	75	74	74	74	74	74	73	73	73	4
5	79	78	78	78	77	77	77	77	77	76	76	76	76	76	76	75	5
6	81	80	80	80	79	79	79	79	78	78	78	78	77	77	77	77	6
7	83	82	82	82	81	81	81	80	80	80	79	79	79	79	79	78	7
8	85	84	84	83	83	83	82	82	82	81	81	81	81	80	80	80	8
9	87	86	86	85	85	84	84	84	83	83	83	82	82	82	81	81	9
10	89	88	88	87	87	86	86	85	85	84	84	84	83	83	83	82	10
11	90	90	89	89	88	88	88	87	87	86	86	85	85	84	84	84	11
12	92	91	91	90	90	89	89	88	88	88	87	87	86	86	86	85	12
13	93	92	92	91	91	91	90	90	89	89	89	88	88	88	87	87	13
14	95	94	93	93	92	92	91	91	90	90	90	89	89	89	88	88	14
15	96	96	95	94	94	93	93	92	92	91	91	90	90	90	89	89	15
16	98	97	97	96	95	95	94	94	93	93	92	92	91	91	90	90	16
17	99	99	98	97	97	96	96	95	95	94	93	93	92	92	92	91	17
18	101	100	99	99	98	98	97	96	96	95	95	94	94	93	93	92	18
19	102	102	101	100	100	99	98	98	97	97	96	96	95	95	94	94	19
20	103	103	102	102	101	100	100	99	99	98	97	97	96	96	95	95	20
21	104	104	103	103	102	102	101	101	100	99	99	98	98	97	97	96	21
22	106	105	105	104	103	103	103	102	101	101	100	100	99	98	98	97	22
23	107	106	106	105	105	104	104	103	103	102	102	101	100	100	99	99	23
24	108	107	107	106	106	105	105	104	104	103	103	102	102	101	101	100	24
25	109	109	108	108	107	107	106	106	105	104	104	103	103	102	102	101	25
26	111	110	110	109	108	108	107	107	106	106	105	105	104	103	103	103	26
27	112	112	111	111	110	109	109	108	107	107	106	106	105	105	104	104	27
28	114	113	113	112	111	111	110	109	109	108	107	107	107	106	105	105	28
29	116	115	114	114	113	112	112	111	110	110	109	108	108	107	107	106	29
30	117	117	116	115	115	114	114	113	112	111	111	110	109	108	108	107	30
31	119	119	118	117	117	116	115	115	114	113	112	112	111	110	109	109	31
32	122	121	120	120	119	118	117	117	116	115	114	114	113	112	111	110	32
33	124	123	123	122	121	120	120	119	118	117	116	116	115	114	113	112	33
34	127	127	125	125	124	123	122	122	121	120	119	118	117	116	115	115	34
35			130	129	128	127	126	125	124	123	122	121	120	119	118	117	35
36								130	129	127	126	125	124	123	122	120	36
37													130	128	126	125	37
38																	38
39																	39
40																	40
	8:9	8:10	8:11	9:0	9:1	9:2	9:3	9:4	9:5	9:6	9:7	9:8	9:9	9:10	9:11	10:0	

PiRA 4 Spring

PiRA 4 Spring standardised scores

Age in years and months

Raw Score	8:0	8:1	8:2	8:3	8:4	8:5	8:6	8:7	8:8	8:9	8:10	8:11	9:0	Raw Score
1														1
2								SCORE 70- IN THIS AREA						2
3	70	70	70	70	70									3
4	73	73	73	73	73	72	72	72	72	72	72	72	72	4
5	77	77	77	76	76	76	76	76	76	76	76	76	76	5
6	80	80	79	79	79	79	79	78	78	78	78	78	78	6
7	82	82	82	81	81	81	81	81	81	80	80	80	80	7
8	84	83	83	83	83	83	82	82	82	82	82	82	82	8
9	85	85	85	84	84	84	84	84	83	83	83	83	83	9
10	87	87	86	86	86	86	85	85	85	85	84	84	84	10
11	89	88	88	88	87	87	87	87	86	86	86	86	85	11
12	90	90	90	90	89	89	89	88	88	88	87	87	87	12
13	92	91	91	91	91	90	90	90	90	89	89	89	88	13
14	93	93	92	92	92	91	91	91	91	91	90	90	90	14
15	95	94	94	94	93	93	92	92	92	92	91	91	91	15
16	96	96	95	95	95	94	94	94	93	93	93	92	92	16
17	97	97	97	96	96	96	95	95	95	94	94	94	93	17
18	99	98	98	98	97	97	97	96	96	96	95	95	95	18
19	100	99	99	99	98	98	98	97	97	97	97	96	96	19
20	101	101	100	100	100	99	99	99	98	98	98	97	97	20
21	102	102	102	101	101	101	100	100	99	99	99	98	98	21
22	104	103	103	102	102	102	101	101	101	100	100	100	99	22
23	105	105	104	104	103	103	103	102	102	102	101	101	101	23
24	107	107	106	106	105	105	104	104	103	103	102	102	102	24
25	109	108	108	107	107	106	106	105	105	104	104	103	103	25
26	110	110	109	109	109	108	108	107	107	106	106	105	105	26
27	112	111	111	111	110	110	109	109	108	108	107	107	106	27
28	113	113	112	112	112	111	111	110	110	110	109	109	108	28
29	115	115	114	114	113	113	112	112	111	111	111	110	110	29
30	117	117	116	116	115	115	114	113	113	112	112	112	111	30
31	119	119	118	118	117	117	116	115	115	114	114	113	113	31
32	122	121	121	120	119	119	118	118	117	116	116	115	115	32
33	125	124	124	123	122	122	121	120	119	119	118	118	117	33
34	128	128	127	126	125	124	124	123	122	122	121	120	119	34
35			131	130	129	128	127	126	126	125	124	123	123	35
36								130	129	129	128	127	126	36
37													130	37
38														38
39					SCORE 130+ IN THIS AREA									39
40														40
	8:0	8:1	8:2	8:3	8:4	8:5	8:6	8:7	8:8	8:9	8:10	8:11	9:0	

PiRA 4 Spring

Age in years and months

Raw Score	9:1	9:2	9:3	9:4	9:5	9:6	9:7	9:8	9:9	9:10	9:11	10:0	10:1	Raw Score
1														1
2														2
3														3
4	72	72	72	72	72	72	72	72	72	72	72	72	72	4
5	76	76	75	75	75	75	75	75	75	75	75	75	75	5
6	78	78	77	77	77	77	77	77	77	77	77	77	77	6
7	80	80	79	79	79	79	79	79	79	79	78	78	78	7
8	81	81	81	81	81	81	81	81	80	80	80	80	80	8
9	83	82	82	82	82	82	82	82	82	82	81	81	81	9
10	84	84	84	83	83	83	83	83	83	83	82	82	82	10
11	85	85	85	85	84	84	84	84	84	84	83	83	83	11
12	87	86	86	86	86	85	85	85	85	85	85	84	84	12
13	88	88	87	87	87	87	86	86	86	86	86	86	85	13
14	90	89	89	89	88	88	88	88	87	87	87	87	86	14
15	91	90	90	90	90	90	89	89	89	88	88	88	88	15
16	92	91	91	91	91	91	90	90	90	90	89	89	89	16
17	93	93	92	92	92	92	91	91	91	91	91	90	90	17
18	94	94	94	93	93	93	92	92	92	92	91	91	91	18
19	96	95	95	95	94	94	94	93	93	93	92	92	92	19
20	97	97	96	96	96	95	95	95	94	94	94	93	93	20
21	98	98	97	97	97	96	96	96	96	95	95	95	94	21
22	99	99	98	98	98	97	97	97	97	96	96	96	95	22
23	100	100	100	99	99	99	98	98	98	97	97	97	97	23
24	101	101	101	100	100	100	99	99	99	98	98	98	98	24
25	103	102	102	102	101	101	101	100	100	100	99	99	99	25
26	104	104	103	103	102	102	102	101	101	101	100	100	100	26
27	106	105	105	104	104	103	103	103	102	102	102	101	101	27
28	108	107	107	106	106	105	105	104	104	103	103	102	102	28
29	109	109	108	108	107	107	106	106	105	105	104	104	103	29
30	111	110	110	110	109	109	108	108	107	107	106	106	105	30
31	112	112	112	111	111	110	110	109	109	108	108	107	107	31
32	114	114	113	113	112	112	111	111	110	110	110	109	109	32
33	116	116	115	115	114	114	113	112	112	112	111	111	110	33
34	119	118	118	117	116	116	115	115	114	113	113	112	112	34
35	122	121	120	119	119	118	118	117	116	116	115	114	114	35
36	125	124	123	123	122	121	120	120	119	118	117	117	116	36
37	129	128	127	126	125	124	124	123	122	121	120	120	119	37
38				131	130	129	128	127	126	125	124	123	122	38
39									130	129	128	127	126	39
40														40
	9:1	9:2	9:3	9:4	9:5	9:6	9:7	9:8	9:9	9:10	9:11	10:0	10:1	

PiRA 4 Summer

Age in years and months

Raw Score	8:3	8:4	8:5	8:6	8:7	8:8	8:9	8:10	8:11	9:0	9:1	9:2	9:3	Raw Score
1														1
2														2
3	71	71	70	70										3
4	74	74	73	73	72	72	71	71	70	70				4
5	77	77	76	76	75	74	74	73	73	72	72	71	71	5
6	80	80	79	78	78	77	77	76	76	75	74	74	73	6
7	83	82	82	81	80	80	79	79	78	77	77	76	76	7
8	85	85	84	83	83	82	82	81	80	80	79	79	78	8
9	87	86	86	85	85	85	84	83	83	82	82	81	81	9
10	89	88	88	87	87	86	86	85	85	85	84	83	83	10
11	90	90	89	89	88	88	87	87	87	86	86	85	85	11
12	92	91	91	90	90	90	89	89	88	88	87	87	86	12
13	93	92	92	92	91	91	91	90	90	89	89	88	88	13
14	94	94	93	93	93	92	92	91	91	91	90	90	90	14
15	95	95	95	94	94	93	93	93	92	92	91	91	91	15
16	97	96	96	95	95	95	94	94	93	93	93	92	92	16
17	98	98	97	97	96	96	95	95	95	94	94	94	93	17
18	100	99	99	98	98	97	97	96	96	95	95	95	94	18
19	101	101	100	100	99	99	98	98	97	97	96	96	95	19
20	103	102	102	101	101	100	99	99	98	98	98	97	97	20
21	104	104	103	103	102	102	101	101	100	99	99	98	98	21
22	106	105	105	104	104	103	103	102	102	101	100	100	99	22
23	107	107	106	105	105	104	104	103	103	103	102	102	101	23
24	109	108	108	107	106	106	105	105	104	104	103	103	103	24
25	110	110	109	109	108	107	107	106	106	105	105	104	104	25
26	112	112	111	110	110	109	109	108	107	107	106	106	105	26
27	114	113	113	112	112	111	110	110	109	108	108	107	107	27
28	116	115	114	114	113	113	112	111	111	110	109	109	108	28
29	119	118	117	116	115	114	114	113	113	112	111	111	110	29
30	122	121	120	119	118	116	115	115	114	114	113	113	112	30
31	125	124	123	122	121	120	119	117	116	115	115	114	114	31
32	129	128	127	125	124	123	122	121	120	118	117	116	115	32
33				129	128	127	125	124	123	122	121	119	118	33
34							129	128	127	125	124	123	122	34
35										129	128	127	125	35
36													130	36
37														37
38					SCORE 130+ IN THIS AREA									38
39														39
40														40
	8:3	8:4	8:5	8:6	8:7	8:8	8:9	8:10	8:11	9:0	9:1	9:2	9:3	

PiRA 4 Summer standardised scores

PiRA 4 Summer

Age in years and months

Raw Score	9:4	9:5	9:6	9:7	9:8	9:9	9:10	9:11	10:0	10:1	10:2	10:3	10:4	Raw Score
1														1
2		SCORE 70- IN THIS AREA												2
3														3
4														4
5	71	70	70											5
6	73	73	72	72	71	71	70	70	70					6
7	75	75	74	74	74	73	73	72	72	71	71	71	70	7
8	78	77	77	76	76	75	75	75	74	74	73	73	72	8
9	80	80	79	79	78	78	77	77	76	76	75	75	75	9
10	82	82	81	81	80	80	79	79	78	78	77	77	77	10
11	84	84	83	83	82	82	81	81	80	80	79	79	78	11
12	86	86	85	85	84	84	83	83	82	82	81	81	80	12
13	87	87	87	86	86	85	85	85	84	84	83	83	82	13
14	89	89	88	88	87	87	87	86	86	85	85	85	84	14
15	90	90	90	89	89	88	88	88	87	87	86	86	86	15
16	92	91	91	91	90	90	89	89	89	88	88	87	87	16
17	93	92	92	92	91	91	91	90	90	90	89	89	88	17
18	94	94	93	93	92	92	92	91	91	91	90	90	90	18
19	95	95	94	94	94	93	93	92	92	92	91	91	91	19
20	96	96	95	95	95	94	94	94	93	93	93	92	92	20
21	97	97	97	96	96	95	95	95	94	94	94	93	93	21
22	99	98	98	97	97	97	96	96	95	95	95	94	94	22
23	100	100	99	99	98	98	97	97	97	96	96	95	95	23
24	102	102	101	100	100	99	99	98	98	97	97	97	96	24
25	103	103	102	102	101	101	100	100	99	99	98	98	97	25
26	105	104	104	103	103	102	102	101	101	100	100	99	99	26
27	106	106	105	105	104	104	103	103	102	102	101	101	100	27
28	108	107	107	106	105	105	104	104	104	103	103	102	102	28
29	109	109	108	108	107	106	106	105	105	104	104	103	103	29
30	111	110	110	109	109	108	108	107	106	106	105	105	104	30
31	113	112	112	111	110	110	109	109	108	107	107	106	106	31
32	115	114	114	113	112	112	111	110	110	109	108	108	107	32
33	117	116	115	115	114	113	113	112	112	111	110	110	109	33
34	121	119	118	117	116	115	115	114	113	113	112	111	111	34
35	124	123	122	121	119	118	117	116	115	115	114	113	113	35
36	128	127	125	124	123	122	120	119	118	117	116	115	114	36
37			130	128	127	125	124	123	122	120	119	118	117	37
38						130	128	127	125	124	123	122	120	38
39							130	128	127	125	124	39
40												130	128	40
	9:4	9:5	9:6	9:7	9:8	9:9	9:10	9:11	10:0	10:1	10:2	10:3	10:4	

PiRA 5 Autumn

PiRA 5 Autumn standardised scores

Age in years and months

Raw Score	8:5	8:6	8:7	8:8	8:9	8:10	8:11	9:0	9:1	9:2	9:3	9:4	9:5	9:6	9:7	9:8	Raw Score
1	75	73	70	70													1
2	82	79	76	74	72	71	70	70	70								2
3	87	85	83	80	79	77	76	76	75	74	73	72	72	72	71	71	3
4	90	88	87	85	83	81	80	79	78	77	76	76	75	75	74	73	4
5	92	91	90	88	87	85	83	82	81	80	79	78	77	77	76	76	5
6	94	93	92	91	89	88	87	85	84	82	81	80	79	79	78	78	6
7	96	95	94	92	91	90	89	88	86	85	84	83	82	81	80	79	7
8	98	97	96	94	93	92	91	90	89	88	86	85	84	83	82	81	8
9	99	98	97	96	95	94	93	92	91	90	89	87	86	85	84	83	9
10	100	100	99	98	97	96	95	93	92	91	90	89	88	87	86	85	10
11	101	101	100	99	98	97	96	95	94	93	92	91	90	89	88	87	11
12	102	102	101	100	100	99	98	97	96	95	94	93	92	91	90	89	12
13	104	103	102	101	101	100	99	98	97	96	95	94	93	92	91	91	13
14	105	104	103	102	102	101	100	100	99	98	97	96	95	94	93	92	14
15	106	105	105	104	103	102	101	101	100	99	98	97	96	95	94	93	15
16	107	106	106	105	104	103	102	102	101	100	100	99	98	97	96	95	16
17	108	108	107	106	106	105	104	103	102	101	101	100	99	98	97	96	17
18	109	109	108	107	107	106	105	104	104	103	102	101	100	100	99	98	18
19	110	110	109	109	108	107	107	106	105	104	103	102	101	101	100	99	19
20	111	111	110	110	109	108	108	107	106	106	105	104	103	102	101	101	20
21	113	112	112	111	110	110	109	108	108	107	106	105	104	103	102	102	21
22	114	113	113	112	112	111	110	110	109	108	107	107	106	105	104	103	22
23	115	115	114	113	113	112	112	111	110	109	109	108	107	106	105	105	23
24	116	116	115	115	114	114	113	112	112	111	110	109	109	108	107	106	24
25	118	117	117	116	116	115	114	114	113	112	112	111	110	109	108	108	25
26	119	118	118	117	117	116	116	115	115	114	113	112	112	111	110	109	26
27	120	120	119	119	118	118	117	117	116	116	115	114	113	112	112	111	27
28	122	121	121	120	120	119	119	118	118	117	117	116	115	114	114	113	28
29	123	123	122	122	122	121	121	120	119	119	118	118	117	116	115	115	29
30	125	124	124	124	123	123	122	122	121	121	120	119	119	118	117	117	30
31	126	126	125	125	125	125	124	124	123	123	122	122	121	120	120	119	31
32	127	127	127	127	126	126	126	126	125	125	124	124	123	123	122	122	32
33	128	128	128	128	128	128	127	127	127	127	126	126	126	125	125	124	33
34	129	129	129	129	129	129	129	129	128	128	128	128	128	127	127	127	34
35						130	130	130	130	130	130	130	130	130	129	129	35
36																	36
37																	37
38																	38
39							SCORE 130+ IN THIS AREA										39
40																	40
	8:5	8:6	8:7	8:8	8:9	8:10	8:11	9:0	9:1	9:2	9:3	9:4	9:5	9:6	9:7	9:8	

PiRA 5 Autumn

Raw Score	9:9	9:10	9:11	10:0	10:1	10:2	10:3	10:4	10:5	10:6	10:7	10:8	10:9	10:10	10:11	11:0	Raw Score
1																	1
2					SCORE 70- IN THIS AREA												2
3	71	70	70	70	70	70	70	70	70								3
4	73	73	72	72	72	72	71	71	71	71	71	71	71	70	70	70	4
5	75	75	75	74	74	73	73	73	73	72	72	72	72	72	72	71	5
6	77	77	76	76	76	75	75	75	74	74	74	73	73	73	73	73	6
7	79	78	78	77	77	77	76	76	76	75	75	75	75	74	74	74	7
8	80	80	79	79	78	78	78	77	77	77	76	76	76	75	75	75	8
9	82	82	81	80	80	79	79	78	78	78	77	77	77	76	76	76	9
10	84	84	83	82	81	81	80	80	79	79	78	78	78	77	77	77	10
11	86	85	85	84	83	82	81	81	80	80	80	79	79	78	78	78	11
12	88	87	86	85	85	84	83	82	82	81	81	80	80	79	79	79	12
13	90	89	88	87	86	85	85	84	83	83	82	81	81	80	80	80	13
14	91	90	89	89	88	87	86	85	85	84	83	83	82	82	81	81	14
15	92	92	91	90	89	88	88	87	86	85	85	84	84	83	82	82	15
16	94	93	92	91	91	90	89	88	88	87	86	86	85	84	84	83	16
17	96	95	94	93	92	91	90	90	89	88	88	87	86	86	85	84	17
18	97	96	95	94	93	92	92	91	90	89	89	88	87	87	86	86	18
19	98	98	97	96	95	94	93	92	91	91	90	89	89	88	87	87	19
20	100	99	98	97	96	95	94	93	93	92	91	90	90	89	89	88	20
21	101	100	99	99	98	97	96	95	94	93	92	92	91	90	90	89	21
22	102	101	101	100	99	98	97	96	95	94	94	93	92	91	91	90	22
23	104	102	102	101	100	99	99	98	97	96	95	94	93	92	92	91	23
24	105	104	103	102	101	101	100	99	98	97	96	95	95	94	93	92	24
25	107	106	105	104	103	102	101	100	100	99	98	97	96	95	94	93	25
26	108	107	106	105	104	103	102	101	101	100	99	98	97	96	95	95	26
27	110	109	108	107	106	105	104	103	102	101	100	100	99	98	97	96	27
28	112	111	110	109	108	107	106	105	103	102	101	101	100	99	98	97	28
29	114	113	112	111	110	109	108	107	105	104	103	102	101	100	100	99	29
30	116	115	114	113	112	111	110	108	107	106	105	104	103	102	101	100	30
31	118	117	116	115	114	113	112	111	109	108	107	106	105	103	102	101	31
32	121	120	119	118	117	116	115	113	112	111	109	108	107	105	104	103	32
33	124	123	122	121	120	119	118	117	115	114	112	111	109	108	106	105	33
34	126	126	125	125	124	123	122	120	119	118	116	114	112	110	109	107	34
35	129	129	128	128	127	127	126	125	124	123	121	119	117	115	112	110	35
36								130	130	130	129	128	126	123	119	116	36
37															128	126	37
38																	38
39																	39
40																	40
	9:9	9:10	9:11	10:0	10:1	10:2	10:3	10:4	10:5	10:6	10:7	10:8	10:9	10:10	10:11	11:0	

PiRA 5 Spring

Age in years and months

Raw Score	9:0	9:1	9:2	9:3	9:4	9:5	9:6	9:7	9:8	9:9	9:10	9:11	10:0	Raw Score
1														1
2														2
3	72	72	72	71	71	71	71	71	71	71	71	71	70	3
4	78	76	75	74	74	73	73	73	73	73	73	73	73	4
5	86	84	82	81	80	79	78	77	77	77	76	76	76	5
6	91	89	87	85	84	83	82	81	80	80	79	79	78	6
7	94	92	91	89	88	86	85	84	83	82	82	81	81	7
8	96	94	93	92	91	90	88	87	85	84	84	83	82	8
9	97	97	95	94	93	92	91	90	88	87	86	85	84	9
10	99	98	97	96	95	94	93	92	91	90	89	87	87	10
11	100	100	98	98	97	96	95	94	93	92	91	90	89	11
12	102	101	100	99	98	97	96	95	94	93	93	92	91	12
13	103	102	101	100	99	98	98	97	96	95	94	93	93	13
14	104	103	102	102	101	100	99	98	97	96	96	95	94	14
15	105	104	104	103	102	101	100	99	98	98	97	96	95	15
16	106	105	105	104	103	102	101	101	100	99	98	97	97	16
17	107	106	106	105	104	104	103	102	101	100	99	98	98	17
18	108	107	107	106	105	105	104	103	102	101	101	100	99	18
19	109	108	108	107	106	106	105	104	103	103	102	101	100	19
20	110	109	109	108	107	107	106	105	104	104	103	102	101	20
21	111	111	110	109	108	108	107	106	105	105	104	103	102	21
22	112	111	111	110	110	109	108	107	107	106	105	104	104	22
23	113	112	112	111	111	110	109	108	108	107	106	105	105	23
24	114	114	113	112	112	111	111	110	109	108	107	107	106	24
25	115	115	114	114	113	112	112	111	110	110	109	108	107	25
26	117	116	116	115	114	114	113	112	112	111	110	109	108	26
27	119	118	117	116	116	115	114	114	113	112	111	111	110	27
28	120	119	119	118	117	117	116	115	114	113	113	112	111	28
29	121	121	120	120	119	119	118	117	116	115	114	113	112	29
30	123	122	122	121	121	120	120	119	118	117	116	115	114	30
31	124	124	123	123	122	122	121	121	120	119	118	117	116	31
32	126	125	125	124	124	124	123	123	122	121	121	120	119	32
33	128	127	127	127	126	126	125	124	124	123	123	122	121	33
34	130	129	129	129	128	128	127	127	126	126	125	124	124	34
35						130	130	130	129	129	129	128	128	127	35
36													130	36
37														37
38						SCORE 130+ IN THIS AREA								38
39														39
40														40
	9:0	9:1	9:2	9:3	9:4	9:5	9:6	9:7	9:8	9:9	9:10	9:11	10:0	

PiRA 5 Spring standardised scores

PiRA 5 Spring

Age in years and months

Raw Score	10:1	10:2	10:3	10:4	10:5	10:6	10:7	10:8	10:9	10:10	10:11	11:0	11:1	Raw Score
1														1
2			SCORE 70- IN THIS AREA											2
3	70	70	70	70	70	70	70	70	70	70	70	70	70	3
4	73	73	73	72	72	72	72	72	72	72	72	72	72	4
5	75	75	75	75	75	75	74	74	74	74	74	74	74	5
6	78	77	77	77	77	76	76	76	76	76	76	75	75	6
7	80	80	79	79	79	78	78	78	77	77	77	77	77	7
8	82	82	81	81	80	80	80	79	79	79	78	78	78	8
9	84	83	83	82	82	82	81	81	81	80	80	80	79	9
10	86	85	84	84	83	83	82	82	82	81	81	81	81	10
11	88	87	86	85	85	84	84	83	83	83	82	82	82	11
12	90	89	88	87	86	86	85	85	84	84	83	83	83	12
13	92	91	90	89	88	87	87	86	85	85	84	84	84	13
14	93	92	92	91	90	89	89	88	87	86	86	85	85	14
15	94	94	93	92	92	91	90	90	89	88	87	87	86	15
16	96	95	94	93	93	92	92	91	90	90	89	88	87	16
17	97	96	95	95	94	93	93	92	92	91	90	90	89	17
18	98	97	97	96	95	94	94	93	93	92	92	91	90	18
19	99	98	98	97	96	96	95	94	94	93	93	92	91	19
20	101	100	99	98	97	97	96	95	95	94	93	93	93	20
21	102	101	100	99	98	98	97	96	96	95	94	94	93	21
22	103	102	101	100	100	99	98	97	97	96	96	95	94	22
23	104	103	102	102	101	100	99	98	98	97	97	96	95	23
24	105	104	104	103	102	101	100	100	99	98	97	97	96	24
25	106	105	105	104	103	102	101	101	100	99	98	98	97	25
26	107	107	106	105	104	103	103	102	101	100	100	99	98	26
27	109	108	107	106	105	105	104	103	102	101	101	100	99	27
28	110	109	108	107	107	106	105	104	103	103	102	101	100	28
29	112	111	110	109	108	107	106	105	105	104	103	102	101	29
30	113	112	112	111	110	109	108	107	106	105	104	103	102	30
31	115	114	113	112	111	110	109	108	107	106	105	104	104	31
32	118	117	115	114	113	112	111	110	109	108	107	106	105	32
33	120	120	118	117	116	114	113	112	111	110	108	107	106	33
34	123	122	121	120	119	118	116	114	113	112	110	109	108	34
35	126	125	124	123	122	121	120	118	116	114	113	111	110	35
36	130	129	129	128	127	125	124	123	121	119	117	115	112	36
37							131	130	128	126	124	121	118	37
38														38
39														39
40														40
	10:1	10:2	10:3	10:4	10:5	10:6	10:7	10:8	10:9	10:10	10:11	11:0	11:1	

PiRA 5 Spring standardised scores

PiRA 5 Summer

PiRA 5 Summer standardised scores

Age in years and months

Raw Score	9:3	9:4	9:5	9:6	9:7	9:8	9:9	9:10	9:11	10:0	10:1	10:2	10:3	Raw Score
1														1
2														2
3														3
4														4
5														5
6	73	73	72	72	72	72	72	71	71	71	71	71	71	6
7	77	76	76	76	75	75	74	74	74	73	73	73	73	7
8	80	80	79	78	78	77	77	76	76	76	75	75	75	8
9	83	82	82	81	80	80	79	79	78	78	77	77	77	9
10	86	85	84	83	83	82	82	81	80	80	79	79	79	10
11	89	88	87	86	85	84	84	83	82	82	81	81	81	11
12	91	90	89	89	88	87	86	85	84	84	83	83	82	12
13	93	93	92	91	90	89	88	88	87	86	85	85	84	13
14	95	94	94	93	92	92	91	90	89	88	87	87	86	14
15	97	96	95	95	94	93	93	92	91	90	90	89	88	15
16	99	98	97	97	96	95	94	93	93	92	92	91	90	16
17	101	100	99	98	97	97	96	95	94	94	93	93	92	17
18	102	102	101	100	99	98	98	97	96	95	95	94	93	18
19	104	103	102	102	101	100	100	99	98	97	96	96	95	19
20	106	105	104	103	103	102	101	101	100	99	98	97	97	20
21	107	106	106	105	104	103	103	102	101	101	100	99	98	21
22	108	108	107	107	106	105	104	103	103	102	102	101	100	22
23	110	109	109	108	107	107	106	105	104	104	103	102	102	23
24	112	111	110	109	109	108	108	107	106	105	105	104	103	24
25	114	113	112	111	110	110	109	108	108	107	106	106	105	25
26	116	115	114	113	113	112	111	110	109	109	108	107	106	26
27	118	117	116	116	115	114	113	112	111	110	109	109	108	27
28	120	119	118	118	117	116	115	114	113	112	111	110	110	28
29	123	122	121	120	119	118	117	117	116	115	114	113	112	29
30	126	125	124	123	122	121	120	119	118	117	116	115	114	30
31	128	127	127	126	125	124	123	122	121	119	119	118	117	31
32		130	129	129	128	127	126	125	124	123	122	120	119	32
33					130	129	128	127	126	125	124	123	33
34									130	129	128	127	126	34
35													130	35
36														36
37														37
38					SCORE 130+ IN THIS AREA									38
39														39
40														40
	9:3	9:4	9:5	9:6	9:7	9:8	9:9	9:10	9:11	10:0	10:1	10:2	10:3	

PiRA 5 Summer

Raw Score	10:4	10:5	10:6	10:7	10:8	10:9	10:10	10:11	11:0	11:1	11:2	11:3	11:4	Raw Score
1														1
2														2
3				SCORE 70- IN THIS AREA										3
4														4
5														5
6	71	71	70	70	70	70	70	70	70	70	70	70	70	6
7	73	72	72	72	72	72	72	72	72	71	71	71	71	7
8	75	74	74	74	74	74	73	73	73	73	73	73	73	8
9	77	76	76	76	75	75	75	75	75	74	74	74	74	9
10	78	78	78	77	77	77	77	76	76	76	76	75	75	10
11	80	80	79	79	79	78	78	78	77	77	77	77	77	11
12	82	81	81	81	80	80	79	79	79	79	78	78	78	12
13	84	83	83	82	82	81	81	81	80	80	80	79	79	13
14	85	85	84	84	83	83	82	82	82	81	81	81	80	14
15	87	87	86	85	85	84	84	83	83	83	82	82	82	15
16	89	89	88	87	87	86	85	85	84	84	84	83	83	16
17	91	91	90	89	88	88	87	87	86	86	85	85	84	17
18	93	92	92	91	90	90	89	88	88	87	87	86	86	18
19	94	94	93	93	92	91	91	90	89	89	88	88	87	19
20	96	95	94	94	93	93	92	92	91	90	90	89	89	20
21	98	97	96	95	95	94	94	93	93	92	91	91	90	21
22	99	98	98	97	96	96	95	94	94	93	93	92	92	22
23	101	100	100	99	98	97	97	96	95	94	94	93	93	23
24	102	102	101	100	100	99	98	97	97	96	95	95	94	24
25	104	103	103	102	101	101	100	99	98	98	97	96	96	25
26	106	105	104	103	103	102	101	101	100	99	98	98	97	26
27	107	107	106	105	104	103	103	102	102	101	100	99	99	27
28	109	108	108	107	106	105	104	104	103	102	102	101	100	28
29	111	110	109	108	108	107	106	105	105	104	103	102	102	29
30	113	112	111	110	109	109	108	107	106	106	105	104	103	30
31	116	115	114	113	112	110	110	109	108	107	107	106	105	31
32	118	117	116	115	114	113	112	111	110	109	108	108	107	32
33	121	120	119	118	117	116	115	114	112	111	110	109	109	33
34	125	124	122	121	120	119	118	116	115	114	113	112	111	34
35	129	127	126	125	124	122	121	119	118	117	116	115	113	35
36		130	129	128	127	125	124	122	121	119	118	117	36
37							130	128	127	125	124	122	120	37
38										130	129	127	125	38
39														39
40														40
	10:4	10:5	10:6	10:7	10:8	10:9	10:10	10:11	11:0	11:1	11:2	11:3	11:4	

PiRA 5 Summer standardised scores

PiRA 6 Autumn

Age in years and months

Raw Score	9:5	9:6	9:7	9:8	9:9	9:10	9:11	10:0	10:1	10:2	10:3	10:4	10:5	10:6	10:7	10:8	Raw Score
1																	1
2																	2
3																	3
4																	4
5																	5
6	72	72	72	71	71	71	71	71	71	71	71	71	71	70	70	70	6
7	75	75	75	74	74	74	74	74	74	74	74	74	74	73	73	73	7
8	80	79	78	78	77	77	77	77	76	76	76	76	76	75	75	75	8
9	83	82	82	81	80	80	79	79	79	78	78	78	77	77	77	77	9
10	86	85	85	84	83	82	82	81	81	80	80	80	79	79	79	78	10
11	88	87	86	86	85	85	84	84	83	83	82	82	81	81	80	80	11
12	89	89	88	88	87	87	86	86	85	85	84	84	83	83	82	82	12
13	91	90	90	89	89	88	88	87	87	86	86	85	85	84	84	84	13
14	93	92	91	91	90	90	89	88	88	88	87	87	86	86	85	85	14
15	94	93	93	92	92	91	90	90	89	89	88	88	88	87	87	86	15
16	96	95	94	94	93	93	92	91	91	90	90	89	89	88	88	88	16
17	98	97	96	95	95	94	93	93	92	92	91	91	90	90	89	89	17
18	99	99	98	97	96	96	95	94	94	93	93	92	91	91	90	90	18
19	101	100	100	99	98	98	97	96	95	94	94	93	93	92	92	91	19
20	102	102	101	101	100	99	99	98	97	96	96	95	94	94	93	93	20
21	104	103	103	102	102	101	100	100	99	98	97	97	96	95	94	94	21
22	105	105	104	104	103	102	102	101	101	100	99	99	98	97	96	95	22
23	107	106	106	105	104	104	103	103	102	102	101	100	100	99	98	97	23
24	109	108	108	107	106	105	105	104	104	103	102	102	101	101	100	99	24
25	111	110	110	109	108	107	107	106	105	105	104	103	103	102	102	101	25
26	113	112	112	111	110	109	109	108	107	106	106	105	104	104	103	102	26
27	115	115	114	113	112	112	111	110	109	109	108	107	106	105	105	104	27
28	118	117	116	115	115	114	113	112	112	111	110	109	108	108	107	106	28
29	121	120	119	119	118	117	116	115	114	113	113	112	111	110	109	108	29
30	123	122	122	121	120	120	119	118	117	116	115	114	114	113	112	111	30
31	125	125	124	124	123	122	122	121	120	120	119	118	117	116	115	114	31
32	128	127	127	126	126	125	124	124	123	123	122	121	120	120	119	117	32
33	130	130	129	129	128	128	127	127	126	125	125	124	123	123	122	121	33
34							130	130	129	129	128	127	127	126	125	125	34
35													130	130	129	129	35
36																	36
37																	37
38					SCORE 130+ IN THIS AREA												38
39																	39
40																	40
	9:5	9:6	9:7	9:8	9:9	9:10	9:11	10:0	10:1	10:2	10:3	10:4	10:5	10:6	10:7	10:8	

PiRA 6 Autumn standardised scores

PiRA 6 Autumn

Age in years and months

Raw Score	10:9	10:10	10:11	11:0	11:1	11:2	11:3	11:4	11:5	11:6	11:7	11:8	11:9	11:10	11:11	12:0	Raw Score
1																	1
2																	2
3																	3
4		SCORE 70- IN THIS AREA															4
5																	5
6	70	70	70	70	70	70	70	70	70	70	70	70	70	70	70	70	6
7	73	73	73	73	73	73	73	73	73	73	73	73	73	73	73	73	7
8	75	75	75	75	75	75	75	75	74	74	74	74	74	74	74	74	8
9	77	76	76	76	76	76	76	76	76	76	75	75	75	75	75	75	9
10	78	78	78	78	77	77	77	77	77	77	77	76	76	76	76	76	10
11	80	79	79	79	79	79	78	78	78	78	78	78	77	77	77	77	11
12	81	81	81	80	80	80	80	79	79	79	79	79	78	78	78	78	12
13	83	83	82	82	82	81	81	81	80	80	80	80	80	79	79	79	13
14	85	84	84	83	83	83	82	82	82	81	81	81	81	80	80	80	14
15	86	86	85	85	85	84	84	83	83	83	82	82	82	81	81	81	15
16	87	87	86	86	86	85	85	85	84	84	84	83	83	83	82	82	16
17	88	88	87	87	87	86	86	86	85	85	85	85	84	84	84	83	17
18	89	89	89	88	88	87	87	87	86	86	86	86	85	85	85	84	18
19	91	90	90	89	89	89	88	88	87	87	87	86	86	86	86	85	19
20	92	91	91	90	90	90	89	89	88	88	88	87	87	87	87	86	20
21	93	93	92	92	91	91	90	90	89	89	89	88	88	88	87	87	21
22	95	94	94	93	93	92	92	91	91	90	90	89	89	89	88	88	22
23	96	96	95	94	94	93	93	92	92	91	91	90	90	90	89	89	23
24	98	98	97	96	95	95	94	94	93	93	92	92	91	91	90	90	24
25	100	100	99	98	97	96	96	95	94	94	93	93	92	92	91	91	25
26	102	101	101	100	99	98	98	97	96	95	95	94	93	93	93	92	26
27	103	103	102	102	101	100	99	99	98	97	96	96	95	94	94	93	27
28	105	105	104	103	103	102	101	100	100	99	98	97	97	96	95	94	28
29	107	107	106	105	104	104	103	102	101	101	100	99	99	98	97	96	29
30	110	109	108	107	106	105	105	104	103	103	102	101	100	100	99	98	30
31	113	112	111	110	109	108	107	106	105	104	104	103	102	101	101	100	31
32	116	115	114	113	112	111	110	109	108	107	106	105	104	103	103	102	32
33	120	119	118	117	116	114	113	112	111	110	109	108	107	105	105	104	33
34	124	123	122	121	120	119	118	116	115	114	112	111	110	109	107	106	34
35	128	127	126	125	124	123	122	121	120	119	117	115	114	112	111	110	35
36				130	129	128	127	126	125	124	123	121	120	118	116	114	36
37										130	129	128	126	125	123	121	37
38																130	38
39																	39
40																	40
	10:9	10:10	10:11	11:0	11:1	11:2	11:3	11:4	11:5	11:6	11:7	11:8	11:9	11:10	11:11	12:0	

PiRA 6 Autumn standardised scores

PiRA 6 Spring

PiRA 6 Spring standardised scores

Age in years and months

Raw Score	10:0	10:1	10:2	10:3	10:4	10:5	10:6	10:7	10:8	10:9	10:10	10:11	11:0	Raw Score
1														1
2	70													2
3	73	72	71	71	70									3
4	76	75	74	73	73	72	71	70	70					4
5	78	77	76	76	75	75	74	73	72	72	71	70	70	5
6	80	79	79	78	77	77	76	76	75	74	74	73	72	6
7	82	81	81	80	79	79	78	78	77	76	76	75	75	7
8	83	83	82	82	81	81	80	80	79	78	78	77	77	8
9	84	84	84	83	83	82	82	81	81	80	80	79	79	9
10	86	85	85	85	84	84	83	83	82	82	82	81	81	10
11	87	87	86	86	85	85	85	84	84	83	83	82	82	11
12	89	88	88	87	87	86	86	86	85	85	84	84	83	12
13	90	89	89	89	88	88	87	87	87	86	86	85	85	13
14	91	90	90	90	89	89	89	88	88	87	87	87	86	14
15	92	92	91	91	91	90	90	89	89	89	88	88	87	15
16	94	93	93	92	92	91	91	91	90	90	89	89	89	16
17	95	95	94	94	93	93	92	92	91	91	91	90	90	17
18	97	96	96	95	95	94	94	93	93	92	92	91	91	18
19	98	98	97	97	96	96	95	95	94	94	93	93	92	19
20	99	99	98	98	98	97	97	96	96	95	95	94	94	20
21	100	100	100	99	99	99	98	98	97	97	96	96	95	21
22	102	101	101	100	100	100	99	99	99	98	98	97	97	22
23	103	103	102	102	102	101	101	100	100	99	99	99	98	23
24	105	104	104	103	103	103	102	102	101	101	100	100	99	24
25	106	106	106	105	105	104	104	103	103	102	102	102	101	25
26	108	108	107	107	106	106	105	105	104	104	103	103	103	26
27	110	109	109	109	108	108	107	107	106	106	105	105	104	27
28	112	111	111	110	110	109	109	109	108	108	107	107	106	28
29	113	113	113	112	112	111	111	110	110	109	109	108	108	29
30	116	115	115	114	114	113	113	112	112	111	111	111	110	30
31	117	117	117	116	116	116	115	115	114	114	113	112	112	31
32	119	119	118	118	118	117	117	117	116	116	115	115	114	32
33	122	121	121	120	120	119	119	119	118	118	118	117	117	33
34	125	124	124	123	123	122	122	121	121	120	120	119	119	34
35	128	127	127	126	126	125	125	124	124	123	123	122	122	35
36			130	130	129	129	128	128	127	127	126	126	125	36
37											130	130	129	37
38														38
39			SCORE 130+ IN THIS AREA											39
40														40
	10:0	10:1	10:2	10:3	10:4	10:5	10:6	10:7	10:8	10:9	10:10	10:11	11:0	

PiRA 6 Spring

Age in years and months

Raw Score	11:1	11:2	11:3	11:4	11:5	11:6	11:7	11:8	11:9	11:10	11:11	12:0	12:1	Raw Score
1														1
2														2
3							SCORE 70- IN THIS AREA							3
4														4
5														5
6	72	71	70	70										6
7	74	73	73	72	71	71	70	70						7
8	76	76	75	74	74	73	73	72	71	71	70	70		8
9	78	78	77	76	76	75	75	74	74	73	72	72	71	9
10	80	79	79	78	78	77	77	76	76	75	75	74	73	10
11	82	81	81	80	80	79	79	78	78	77	76	76	75	11
12	83	83	82	82	81	81	80	80	79	79	78	78	77	12
13	84	84	83	83	83	82	82	81	81	81	80	80	79	13
14	86	85	85	84	84	83	83	83	82	82	82	81	81	14
15	87	87	86	86	85	85	84	84	84	83	83	82	82	15
16	88	88	87	87	87	86	86	85	85	84	84	84	83	16
17	89	89	89	88	88	88	87	87	86	86	85	85	84	17
18	91	90	90	89	89	89	88	88	88	87	87	86	86	18
19	92	91	91	91	90	90	89	89	89	88	88	88	87	19
20	93	93	92	92	92	91	91	90	90	89	89	89	88	20
21	95	94	94	93	93	92	92	92	91	91	90	90	89	21
22	96	96	95	95	94	94	93	93	92	92	92	91	91	22
23	98	97	97	96	96	96	95	94	94	93	93	93	92	23
24	99	99	98	98	98	97	97	96	96	95	95	94	94	24
25	100	100	100	99	99	98	98	98	97	97	96	96	95	25
26	102	102	101	101	100	100	99	99	99	98	98	97	97	26
27	104	103	103	102	102	101	101	100	100	99	99	99	98	27
28	106	105	105	104	103	103	103	102	102	101	100	100	100	28
29	107	107	107	106	105	105	104	104	103	103	102	102	101	29
30	110	109	108	108	107	107	106	106	105	105	104	104	103	30
31	112	111	111	110	110	109	108	108	107	107	106	106	105	31
32	114	113	113	112	112	111	111	110	110	109	108	108	107	32
33	116	116	115	115	114	114	113	112	112	111	111	110	110	33
34	118	118	118	117	117	116	116	115	115	114	113	113	112	34
35	121	121	120	119	119	119	118	118	117	117	116	116	115	35
36	125	124	124	123	123	122	121	121	120	119	119	118	118	36
37	129	128	128	127	127	126	125	125	124	123	123	122	121	37
38						130	130	129	129	128	127	127	126	38
39														39
40														40
	11:1	11:2	11:3	11:4	11:5	11:6	11:7	11:8	11:9	11:10	11:11	12:0	12:1	

PiRA 6 Spring standardised scores

PiRA 6 Summer

PiRA 6 Summer standardised scores

Raw Score	10:3	10:4	10:5	10:6	10:7	10:8	10:9	10:10	10:11	11:0	11:1	11:2	11:3	Raw Score
1														1
2														2
3														3
4														4
5														5
6														6
7	71	71	71	71	71	71	71	71	71	71	71	70	70	7
8	74	74	74	74	74	73	73	73	73	73	73	73	72	8
9	77	77	77	76	76	76	76	75	75	75	75	75	75	9
10	80	79	79	79	78	78	78	78	77	77	77	77	77	10
11	82	82	81	81	81	80	80	80	80	79	79	79	78	11
12	85	84	84	84	83	83	82	82	82	81	81	81	80	12
13	87	86	86	86	85	85	85	84	84	84	83	83	83	13
14	89	89	88	88	87	87	86	86	86	85	85	85	85	14
15	91	91	91	90	90	89	89	88	88	87	87	87	86	15
16	93	93	92	92	92	91	91	90	90	90	89	89	88	16
17	95	95	94	94	93	93	93	92	92	91	91	91	90	17
18	97	96	96	95	95	95	94	94	94	93	93	92	92	18
19	98	98	97	97	97	96	96	96	95	95	94	94	94	19
20	100	99	99	99	98	98	98	97	97	96	96	96	95	20
21	102	102	101	100	100	100	99	99	98	98	98	97	97	21
22	104	104	103	103	102	102	101	100	100	100	99	99	98	22
23	106	105	105	104	104	104	103	103	102	102	101	100	100	23
24	107	107	107	106	106	105	105	104	104	104	103	103	102	24
25	109	109	108	108	108	107	107	106	106	105	105	104	104	25
26	111	111	110	110	109	109	108	108	108	107	107	106	106	26
27	114	113	113	112	112	111	110	110	109	109	109	108	108	27
28	116	115	115	114	114	113	113	112	112	111	111	110	110	28
29	118	117	117	116	116	115	115	115	114	114	113	113	112	29
30	120	119	119	119	118	118	117	117	116	116	115	115	114	30
31	123	122	122	121	121	120	120	119	119	118	118	117	117	31
32	125	125	124	124	123	123	122	122	121	121	120	120	119	32
33	129	128	128	127	127	126	125	125	124	124	123	123	122	33
34				130	130	129	129	128	128	127	127	126	125	34
35											130	130	129	35
36														36
37														37
38							SCORE 130+ IN THIS AREA							38
39														39
40														40
	10:3	10:4	10:5	10:6	10:7	10:8	10:9	10:10	10:11	11:0	11:1	11:2	11:3	

PiRA 6 Summer

Age in years and months

Raw Score	11:4	11:5	11:6	11:7	11:8	11:9	11:10	11:11	12:0	12:1	12:2	12:3	12:4	Raw Score
1														1
2														2
3				SCORE 70- IN THIS AREA										3
4														4
5														5
6														6
7	70	70	70	70	70	70	70	70	70	70	70	70	70	7
8	72	72	72	72	72	72	72	72	72	72	72	71	71	8
9	74	74	74	74	74	74	74	73	73	73	73	73	73	9
10	76	76	76	76	76	75	75	75	75	75	75	75	75	10
11	78	78	78	78	77	77	77	77	77	77	76	76	76	11
12	80	80	80	79	79	79	79	79	78	78	78	78	78	12
13	82	82	82	81	81	81	80	80	80	80	80	79	79	13
14	84	84	84	83	83	83	82	82	82	81	81	81	81	14
15	86	86	85	85	85	85	84	84	84	83	83	83	82	15
16	88	87	87	87	86	86	86	85	85	85	85	84	84	16
17	90	90	89	89	88	88	87	87	87	86	86	86	86	17
18	92	91	91	91	90	90	89	89	89	88	88	87	87	18
19	93	93	92	92	92	91	91	91	90	90	90	89	89	19
20	95	95	94	94	93	93	93	92	92	92	91	91	91	20
21	96	96	96	95	95	95	94	94	94	93	93	92	92	21
22	98	98	97	97	96	96	96	95	95	95	94	94	94	22
23	100	99	99	98	98	98	97	97	97	96	96	95	95	23
24	102	101	100	100	100	99	99	98	98	98	97	97	97	24
25	104	103	103	102	102	101	101	100	100	99	99	98	98	25
26	105	105	105	104	104	103	103	102	102	101	101	100	100	26
27	107	107	106	106	105	105	105	104	104	103	103	102	102	27
28	109	109	108	108	107	107	106	106	105	105	105	104	104	28
29	111	111	110	110	109	109	108	108	107	107	106	106	106	29
30	114	113	113	112	112	111	110	110	109	109	108	108	107	30
31	116	116	115	115	114	114	113	113	112	111	111	110	109	31
32	119	118	118	117	117	116	115	115	114	114	113	113	112	32
33	122	121	120	120	119	119	118	117	117	116	116	115	115	33
34	125	124	124	123	122	122	121	120	120	119	119	118	117	34
35	129	128	127	127	126	125	125	124	123	123	122	121	121	35
36					130	129	129	128	127	127	126	125	124	36
37												130	129	37
38														38
39														39
40														40
	11:4	11:5	11:6	11:7	11:8	11:9	11:10	11:11	12:0	12:1	12:2	12:3	12:4	

PiRA 6 Summer standardised scores

Appendix A: Levels of demand and AF coverage for each test

PiRA 6 Autumn

NC Level	AF 2	AF 3	AF 4	AF 5	AF 6	AF 7	
5a							
5b							
5c			2			2	
			2				2
4a		3		4	3		10
4b	3	1			2	1	7
4c	2	2	1				5
	5	6	1	4	5	1	22
3a		4	1	1	1		7
3b	1	2		1			4
3c	4	1					5
2a							
	5	7	1	2	1		16
	10	13	4	6	6	1	40

PiRA 6 Spring

NC Level	AF 2	AF 3	AF 4	AF 5	AF 6	AF 7	
5a							
5b				2			2
5c				1			1
				3			3
4a	2	2		1			5
4b		4		3	1	3	11
4c	1	2	1	3	3		10
	3	8	1	7	4	3	26
3a		3					3
3b	3	2		1			6
3c	2						2
	5	5		1			11
	8	13	1	11	4	3	40

PiRA 6 Summer

NC Level	AF 2	AF 3	AF 4	AF 5	AF 6	AF 7	
5a							
5b		2	2			4	
5c			2	2	1	5	
		2	4	2	1	9	
4a	1	2			1		4
4b	1	6		1		2	10
4c		3		3	1		7
	2	11		4	2	2	21
3a	2	1					3
3b	3						3
3c	3				1		4
2a							
	8	1			1		10
	10	14	4	6	4	2	40

PiRA 5 Autumn

NC Level	AF 2	AF 3	AF 4	AF 5	AF 6	AF 7	
5c			1				1
		1					1
4a		1					1
4b	1	1					2
4c		4		3		2	9
	1	6		3		2	12
3a		4		2			6
3b	3	2	2	3		1	11
3c	1	3	1	1			6
	4	9	3	6		1	23
2a	3	1					4
2b							
	3	1					4
	8	16	4	9		3	40

PiRA 5 Spring

NC Level	AF 2	AF 3	AF 4	AF 5	AF 6	AF 7	
5c				3			3
				3			3
4a			2	1			3
4b		3			1	2	6
4c		4	3				7
		7	5	2	2		16
3a	8	2					10
3b		2	1	2	2		7
3c		2					2
	8	6	1	2	2		19
2a	1		1				2
2b							
	1		1				2
	9	13	2	7	7	2	40

PiRA 5 Summer

NC Level	AF 2	AF 3	AF 4	AF 5	AF 6	AF 7	
5c			3				3
			3				3
4a			4	2		2	8
4b		2	1	2	2		7
4c		6		1			7
		8	5	5	2	2	22
3a	2	1					3
3b	4	4					8
3c	3						3
	9	5					14
2a	1						1
2b							
	1						1
	10	13	8	5	2	2	40

PiRA 4 Autumn

NC Level	AF 2	AF 3	AF 4	AF 5	AF 6	AF 7	
4a							
4b			1	1			2
4c		4		1			5
		4	1	2			7
3a		2	1				3
3b	1	3	2			1	7
3c	1	2			1	2	6
	2	7	3		1	3	16
2a	4	3	1	1			9
2b	3			3			6
2c		1					1
1a	1						1
	8	4	1	4			17
	10	15	5	6	1	3	40

PiRA 4 Spring

NC Level	AF 2	AF 3	AF 4	AF 5	AF 6	AF 7	
4a		1		1			2
4b		2				2	4
4c		1	2		1		4
		4	2	1	1	2	10
3a	1	1	1	1	1	1	6
3b		5		1			6
3c	1	3	2	2	1		9
	2	9	3	4	2	1	21
2a	2			1			3
2b	2	1		2			5
2c	1						1
	5	1		2	1		9
	7	14	5	7	4	3	40

PiRA 4 Summer

NC Level	AF 2	AF 3	AF 4	AF 5	AF 6	AF 7	
4a		1			2		3
4b		1					1
4c	2	3			1		6
	2	5			3		10
3a			3	3		3	9
3b	2	2	2	1	1		8
3c	1	2		2			5
	3	4	5	6	1	3	22
2a	4	1			1		6
2b	1	1					3
2c							
	5	2			1		9
	10	11	5	6	4	4	40

NC Level	AF1	AF2	AF3	AF4	AF5	AF6	AF7		NC Level	AF1	AF2	AF3	AF4	AF5	AF6	AF7		NC Level	AF1	AF2	AF3	AF4	AF5	AF6	AF7	
\multicolumn{9}{c	}{PiRA 3 Autumn}	\multicolumn{9}{c	}{PiRA 3 Spring}	\multicolumn{9}{c}{PiRA 3 Summer}
4c									4c			2				2	2	4c			3	1			4	4
												2				2	2				3	1			4	4
3a			2	1				3	3a			2				2	2	3a			3	1			4	4
3b			2	1				3	3b			4	3	1		8	8	3b		1	3	1	1	2		8
3c		1	3		1			5	3c		1	3	2	1	1	8	8	3c		4	3	1	1			9
		1	7	2	1			11			1	7	7	2	1	18	18			5	9	2	3	2		21
2a		1	2	3	1			7	2a			2		2		4	4	2a		1	4			1		6
2b		1	2		1		1	5	2b	2		1				3	3	2b	1	2	1		1			5
2c	2	4		1		1		8	2c	1	6	1				7	7	2c		2						2
	2	6	4	4	2	1	1	20		3	6	3		2		14	14		1	5	5		1		1	13
1a	2	3						5	1a		3	1				4	4	1a		1						1
1b	2	2						4	1b				2			2	2	1b	1							1
1c									1c									1c								
	4	5						9			3	1	2			6	6		1	1						2
	6	12	11	6	3	1	1	40		3	10	13	9	4	1	40	40		2	12	16	3	4	2	1	40

The 'assessment focuses' for reading:

AF1 – decoding text
AF2 – literal understanding and retrieval from text
AF3 – inference and prediction from text
AF4 – appreciating structure and organisation of text, including presentational features
AF5 – appreciating writer's use of language, including grammatical and literary features at word and sentence level
AF6 – appreciating writer's purpose and viewpoint
AF7 – appreciating social, cultural and historical context and literary tradition

Appendix B: Facilities for each question

PiRA 3 Autumn	% correct	PiRA 4 Autumn	% correct	PiRA 5 Autumn	% correct	PiRA 6 Autumn	% correct
Q1	80	Q1	90	Q1 70	81	Q1	52
Q2 1 or 2	94	Q2	62	Q1 2 37	78	Q2 true	75
Q2 3 or 4	91	Q3	79	Q2	63	Q2 false	81
Q3	68	Q4	76	Q3	66	Q3 float	72
Q4	47	Q5	40	Q4	53	Q3 paddle	63
Q5	41	Q6A book	45	Q5	39	Q4 puff	59
Q6	44	Q6B read	42	Q6 immersed	57	Q4 red	59
Q7	64	Q7	56	Q6 submerged	49	Q5	46
Q8	66	Q8A	67	Q7 true1	50	Q6	47
Q9	71	Q8B dirt	39	Q7 true2	37	Q7	77
Q10	51	Q8B smell	28	Q7 false	50	Q8	39
Q11	50	Q9	50	Q8 1926	69	Q9	68
Q11	73	Q10	32	Q8 1904	75	Q10 speed	50
Q12	45	Q11	18	Q8 1908	77	Q10 move	65
Q13	47	Q12	33	Q9 exhausted	36	Q11 absorb	36
Q14	76	Q13	61	Q9 panicked	41	Q11 hypno	37
Q15	67	Q14	52	Q10	34	Q12 imag	74
Q16A	57	Q15	64	Q11	29	Q12 underst	62
Q16B	76	Q16	48	Q12 evac	47	Q13 signal	70
Q17	28	Q17	51	Q12 tranq	35	Q13 change	55
Q18	56	Q18 1 or 2	56	Q13	56	Q14	62
Q19	71	Q18 all 3	41	Q14 attck	56	Q15	75
Q20	69	Q19	31	Q14 dead	45	Q16	39
Q21	67	Q20	53	Q15 sub	44	Q17 talk	35
Q22	67	Q21 1 or 2	57	Q15 quote	51	Q17 panic	55
Q23	42	Q21 3 or 4	32	Q16 1 or 2	50	Q17 pred	54
Q24	32	Q22 1 or 2	46	Q16 3 or 4	34	Q18	46
Q25 help	60	Q22 all 3	30	Q17	51	Q19 true	80
Q25 see	48	Q23	28	Q18	57	Q19 false	41
Q26	55	Q24	34	Q19	36	Q19 DNS	33
Q27	51	Q25 eyes	54	Q20	29	Q20 1 or 2	91
Q28 any 2	30	Q25 skies	55	Q21	32	Q20 3 or 4	74
Q28 all 4	24	Q25 sighs	48	Q22	58	Q21 1 or 2	90
Q29	74	Q26	33	Q23	30	Q21 3 or 4	68
Q30 glum	66	Q27 jockey	41	Q24A	38	Q22	68
Q30 chum	60	Q27 thief	37	Q24B	28	Q23	74
Q31	58	Q28	39	Q25	50	Q24	65
Q32	29	Q29	20	Q26A	68	Q25	39
Q33 alright	33	Q30	18	Q26B danger	48	Q26	44
Q33 hurt	42	Q31	27	Q26B exc	55	Q27	37

PiRA 3 Spring	% correct	PiRA 4 Spring	% correct	PiRA 5 Spring	% correct	PiRA 6 Spring	% correct
Q1A	88	Q1	88	Q	65	Q1	78
Q1B	77	Q2	83	Q	53	Q2A	83
Q2	85	Q3	64	Q3A	81	Q2B	60
Q3	60	Q4	43	Q3B	72	Q3	49
Q4	71	Q5	67	Q4	60	Q4	75
Q5	37	Q6 false1	76	Q5	39	Q5	43
Q6 3 or 4	35	Q6 false2	69	Q6	91	Q6A	52
Q7	28	Q6 DNS	57	Q7	64	Q6B	38
Q8 3	80	Q7 head	60	Q8 any 1	49	Q7	44
Q9	80	Q7 label	46	Q8 any 2	43	Q8	55
Q10	71	Q8	56	Q9	34	Q9	87
Q11	80	Q9 exclam	41	Q10	64	Q10	78
Q12	84	Q9 allit	40	Q11 3 4	76	Q11A	78
Q13 3 or 4	76	Q10	38	Q11 5 6	35	Q11B	69
Q14	57	Q11	59	Q12 happy	42	Q12	82
Q15	38	Q12 bath	37	Q12 sad	26	Q13	82
Q16	69	Q12 carpet	35	Q13	49	Q14	51
Q17	34	Q13	75	Q14	49	Q15	66
Q18	46	Q14	32	Q15A	35	Q16 loud	73
Q19	71	Q15	65	Q15B	23	Q16 quiet	63
Q20	32	Q16A But …	33	Q16	62	Q17 allit	60
Q21	14	Q16B noise	65	Q17 wings	39	Q17 simile	43
Q22	72	Q17 relax	63	Q17 head	39	Q18	71
Q23	60	Q17 scared	53	Q18	31	Q19	54
Q24	55	Q18	72	Q19 mount	40	Q20 1 or 2	79
Q25	78	Q19 4 or 5	26	Q19 river	39	Q20 3 or 4	29
Q26 4	72	Q20	43	Q20 good	69	Q21 dumb	54
Q27	37	Q21	38	Q20 nature	35	Q21 primi	30
Q28	25	Q22	58	Q21	41	Q22	31
Q29 2 or 3	30	Q23	68	Q22	68	Q23A	70
Q30	70	Q24	59	Q23F	31	Q23B	58
Q31	11	Q25	17	Q24 any 4	59	Q23C	37
Q32	43	Q26	74	Q24 all 6	29	Q24 3 or 4	57
Q33	25	Q27 feeling	67	Q25 comp	38	Q25	43
Q33	29	Q27 wings	58	Q25 know	53	Q26 explode	42
Q33	26	Q28	45	Q26 rare	38	Q26 riot	39
Q34	33	Q29	24	Q26 dino	35	Q27	18
Q35 safe	71	Q30	65	Q27 report	27	Q28 trans	76
Q35 fun	40	Q31 2 or 3	60	Q27 poem	40	Q28 Merlin	61
Q36 2 or 3	38	Q31 all	12	Q27 myth	33	Q28 lesson	40

Appendix B: Facilities for each question

PiRA 3 Summer	% correct	PiRA 4 Summer	% correct	PiRA 5 Summer	% correct	PiRA 6 Summer	% correct
Q1	92	Q1	57	Q1	92	Q1	91
Q2	83	Q2	66	Q2	87	Q2	81
Q3	71	Q3	77	Q3	49	Q3	41
Q4	84	Q4	52	Q4	40	Q4	78
Q5 1 or 2	85	Q5 any 1	73	Q5	39	Q5 2 or 3	66
Q5 3 or 4	46	Q5 any 1	69	Q6	67	Q5 4+	48
Q6	53	Q5 any 1	67	Q7	34	Q5	24
Q7	72	Q6	55	Q8	80	Q6	74
Q8 queen	72	Q7	65	Q9	15	Q6	48
Q8 grubs	57	Q8	68	Q10	52	Q7	52
Q8 worker	50	Q9	43	Q11 2 or 3	89	Q8 any 1	74
Q9	49	Q10A	63	Q11 4 or 5	80	Q8 2nd	64
Q10	62	Q10B	50	Q12 1 or 2	73	Q9 both	19
Q11	87	Q11	86	Q12 3 or 4	48	Q10	63
Q12A	73	Q12	81	Q13A	71	Q11	50
Q12B	31	Q13	37	Q13B his own	46	Q12	44
Q13	41	Q14	55	Q13B blood	47	Q13	43
Q14	45	Q15 Jim	39	Q14 threat	42	Q14 any 2	57
Q15	48	Q15 Sandy	21	Q14 polite	25	Q14 all 3	39
Q16	51	Q16	32	Q15	72	Q15 any 2	49
Q17	65	Q17A	62	Q16	51	Q15 all 4	31
Q18	58	Q17B	74	Q17	32	Q16 any 2	52
Q19	79	Q18A	70	Q18 2 or 3	83	Q16 all 3	35
Q20	34	Q18B	48	Q18 4 or 5	60	Q17	60
Q21	71	Q19	37	Q19 12	40	Q18 any 2	87
Q22A	78	Q20	48	Q19 45	24	Q18 any 4	82
Q22B	54	Q21	52	Q19 3	36	Q18 all 6	38
Q23	72	Q22	57	Q20	54	Q19 dont	56
Q24	79	Q23	72	Q21	46	Q19 true 1	58
Q25	59	Q24	49	Q22	64	Q19 true 2	31
Q26	51	Q25 new	69	Q23	50	Q20 manner	58
Q27	66	Q25 no sp	45	Q24 2 or 3	82	Q20 gift	51
Q28	34	Q25 instr	48	Q24 4 or 5	58	Q20 rules	54
Q29	32	Q26	42	Q25 rhyme	53	Q21	35
Q30	15	Q27	35	Q25 engage	31	Q22 any 3	58
Q30	61	Q28	37	Q26 1 or 2	67	Q22 all 4	44
Q31	27	Q29	42	Q26 3 or 4	39	Q23	28
Q32	53	Q30 1 or 2	66	Q27 inform	49	Q24	28
Q32	14	Q30 all 3	9	Q27 person	24	Q25 any 2	52
Q33	10	Q33	38	Q28 2 or 3	54	Q25 all 3	35

Appendix B: Facilities for each question

PiRA Appendix C: Mean marks by sub-level

In the standardisation trials teacher-assessment (TA) information was provided by teachers using their professional judgement of the levels of the pupils when they took the tests.

As may be expected, the TA-generated mean marks in autumn are slightly lower than the marks obtained by equating to the Optional or Key Stage tests taken in the previous summer. This makes a TA-generated level more accessible. The main reason is that the pupils in autumn are almost one term on from when they took the Optional and Key Stage tests.

The TA levels were used to provide the basis for all the equating in the spring term, as links back to the previous summer are inappropriate – as indeed would be links forward to the following summer national-test derived levels. The summer term comparison of TA sub-level and national-test derived sub-level indicated that teachers, on the whole, are a little more generous with the more and least able.

NC sub-level	Autumn PiRA 3	Autumn PiRA 4	Autumn PiRA 5	Autumn PiRA 6	Spring PiRA 3	Spring PiRA 4	Spring PiRA 5	Spring PiRA 6	Summer PiRA 3	Summer PiRA 4	Summer PiRA 5	Summer PiRA 6
5a				35				35				33
5b			35	33			34	32			33	29
5c			32	30			32	29		35	30	25
4a			30	27		32	28	26		32	28	22
4b		32	27	26		32	24	23		30	25	21
4c		30	24	23	36	30	20	20	33	28	21	18
3a		26	20	20	33	26	16	15	30	24	19	16
3b	34	21	17	16	31	23	13	14	28	22	16	13
3c	32	18	14	14	28	18	11	9	24	16	13	12
2a	27	14	11	10	23	14	7	7	20	12	11	12
2b	22	11	8		18	10	6	5	15	11	4	12
2c	16	8			11	7	5		12	7		12
1a	9	7			8	6	4		6	5		7
1b	6	3			5	7			5			
1c	5				6				4			

The close relationship of mean mark from TA and equated mark from national tests, for each sub-level, further supports the validity and reliability of the *PiRA* tests.